W9-AEE-617

MODERN CHINA
A BRIEF HISTORY

DAVID NELSON ROWE
Professor of Political Science
Yale University

AN ANVIL ORIGINAL
under the general editorship of
LOUIS L. SNYDER

D. VAN NOSTRAND COMPANY, INC.
PRINCETON, NEW JERSEY
TORONTO   LONDON
NEW YORK

IN RESPECTFUL MEMORY OF
HARLEY FARNSWORTH MacNAIR

D. VAN NOSTRAND COMPANY, INC.

120 Alexander St., Princeton, New Jersey (*Principal office*)

257 Fourth Avenue, New York 10, New York

25 Hollinger Rd., Toronto 16, Canada

358, Kensington High Street, London, W.14, England

Library of Congress Catalog Card No. 59-15095

PREFACE

The gigantic movements and cataclysmic events of modern Chinese history are difficult to compress within a summary of about one hundred printed pages of text and an equal quantity of documents. A great deal of selection is forced upon anyone so bold as to attempt thus to present China's course of development during the past century and more. Accordingly, the author has chosen to emphasize the more recent developments, at the same time providing a briefer coverage of the period from 1839 to 1895.

The most recent 120 years of China's history are in many ways highly different from anything in China's more remote past. And yet China, even today, when in the throes of a total revolution on the mainland, is tied inextricably to that remoter past, and this tie has in many ways shaped and determined the revolutionary events of the present day.

Accordingly, those who seek fundamental understanding of China in recent times are urged to study her past traditions as embodied in her recorded history of nearly 3,500 years. In the United States, and in the West in general, the study of that history is still in its infancy. But perhaps what has happened in China in recent decades has begun at last to convince us that we cannot continue to disregard the human record in China, Chinese history, much longer. If we do, we have only ourselves to blame if our ignorance of China leads us in the direction of national disaster.

If this small volume succeeds in any way in arousing a more general interest in the study of China, it will have achieved its author's greatest hope.

DAVID NELSON ROWE

TABLE OF CONTENTS

Part 1

MODERN CHINA

— 1 —

THE DECAY OF IMPERIAL CHINA

The People and Their Country. The ancient land of China includes a total area of some 1,500,000 square miles, stretching from Manchuria in the northeast to Tibet in the southwest and from the island of Taiwan (Formosa) in the South China Sea northwestward to Chinese Turkestan in central Asia. Much of this territory consists of very high mountains and dry, sandy deserts. Of the remainder, much is too hilly for farming, so that of the total area only about twenty-five per cent can be cultivated. Here the climate is generally temperate, and it is in this part of the country lying for the most part in the east, center, and southeast, that the Chinese have lived for so many centuries.

As far as can be discovered, the original home of Chinese civilization was in the lower part of the Yellow River valley. From here it spread out to much of east Asia and had its powerful influences upon the cultures of neighboring non-Chinese peoples, such as the Japanese and Koreans. In the process of spreading south and east from North China, the Chinese people slowly but irresistibly pushed aside other peoples of alien cultures. They took the valleys and the lower hills and put them under cultivation. The aboriginal peoples retreated into the higher mountains where many of them exist today. There are still some 20,000,000 of these non-Chinese people in China, loosely organized in tribes and still a problem to Chinese regimes which in modern times have tried to absorb them culturally or to bring them under the authority of government.

The Chinese population itself has increased, particularly during recent centuries, until today it probably numbers some 600,000,000 the largest population of any single political entity in the world. This huge population is in itself the source of many problems, some seemingly almost insoluble. It is still increasing, and by a net total of some 12,000,000 per year. Since most, if not all, of the cultivatable land is already under intense farming and producing to the maximum under present conditions, a genuine revolution in agriculture will be necessary even to keep up with the current population increases. But what will be the source of the capital necessary for such a revolution in agricultural technique, especially since agriculture is itself the main source of China's income and is insufficient even to feed China's people, let alone as a source of savings for capital?

In addition, the massive Chinese population suffers from very low levels of health and education. And, aside from agricultural land, the natural resources of the country are not at all rich, especially when averaged out per capita. Under the circumstances it is not too surprising, perhaps, to find that modern China has been and still is a country where those in power have attempted some of the most extreme and drastic measures of control ever applied to great numbers of human beings at one time. In spite of this, the main problems of the Chinese people have hardly been touched by any of the numerous governments that have succeeded each other in the last 100 years.

The Social Inheritance. The wonder is, indeed, that China still survives today. It probably could not, if it were not for its cultural and social inheritance from the past. This inheritance includes a number of elements seemingly in contradiction with each other, but which actually embody a genuine harmony of opposites. For example, a thousand and more years ago China was already a state in which there existed a single unified government. This government ruled over a country of such large area and primitive communications as seemingly to make impractical a centralized governing authority. This contradiction was resolved by allowing most of the governing to be done on the village and family level, loosely supervised by a bureaucracy sent out from the imperial capital. Thus the Chinese "empire" was unlike that of Rome in which vast territories, inhabited by alien peoples, were ruled as colonies by Roman overlords. Great

China, with the exception of the aborigines in the higher mountains, was culturally unified; it was Chinese.

When, throughout the centuries, local variations of the spoken language grew up, the Chinese had the advantage always of their uniform written script. This script was, and is, ideographic, not phonetic. Since it renders ideas, and does not spell out sounds, it is proof against any and all variations in pronunciation of words from time to time and place to place. In this script, therefore, have come down to the present the great ideas that have bound the Chinese people together for so long a part of human history. Thus cultural entity was preserved through time. And, since the script was also proof against change through pronunciation of the language from place to place in the huge area of China, it preserved China's cultural unity in space as well.

In this way, among others, China has resisted political fragmentation, the fate of most early empires spread out over large geographical areas. She has broken apart numerous times in the past, but political fragmentation has always had to surrender to cultural unity.

The Scholar-Bureaucrats. In the preservation of this cultural unity a relatively small part of the people played a disproportionately important part. These were the educated minority, persons learned in the traditions handed down from the past. They were influential not only as custodians of the cultural inheritance, but as local governors on behalf of the imperial monarchy. Government in imperial China, as in other places, depended in very early times on the keeping of written records, the embodiment in written form of the precedents and experiences of the political process. Thus skills in reading (for the inheritance from the past) and writing (for the processes of the present) were necessary for the conduct of government. The numbers of those possessing these skills were kept small by the necessity for the learned man to memorize large numbers of the ideographs that made up the written language. The resultant virtual monopoly of learning in the hands of a few might seem to have been a handicap to efficient government, by preventing easy communication through the large territory of China. On the other hand, however, it facilitated ideological control and promoted cultural unity by keeping control of affairs in the hands of a small minority who had a real stake in the unity of their class and the preservation of its privileged status.

Although these scholar-bureaucrats were a class, they were not a caste. They entered government after passing examinations in classics and literature. Since governmental power gave them economic advantage, their own sons could afford education and tended to follow after them in the same careers. But under normal circumstances there would always be a number of newcomers in the ranks, young men who, however obscure their origins, had managed through the sacrifices of their relatives to secure an education, and who on entry into the ranks of officialdom were expected to bring not only honor, but financial rewards, to their families and relatives.

These bureaucrats and administrators scattered through the empire were never very numerous. No great numbers were required for the normal operation of the central administration in the provinces. Here we see another of the seeming contradictions of traditional Chinese society. The imperial government was at the same time absolutist but relatively weak, despotic but not totalitarian. Overwhelmingly, the government which affected the daily life of the peasants was local in origin and application. For the most part it was familial; the village was governed by the village elders, the oldest male members of the clan. In many villages, all inhabitants were of the same family, they all had the same surname. Over these people the village elders governed in a paternalistic way, enforcing custom with the force of law, and having in the most extreme cases the power of life and death over the villagers. The elders also represented the village in its relationship to the more immediate aspects of central government, embodied in the magistrates whose main functions were the preservation of general order and the collection of taxes on behalf of higher authority.

The village elders were, indeed, responsible to the higher authorities of government under a general system of collective responsibility. Crime, for instance, might be committed by individuals, but the responsibility for it was collective. In case the guilty party could not be found, punishment could be imposed upon his entire family or village. This type of thing tended to make anybody's business the business of everybody. Nobody could live in privacy under such a system, and, indeed, the very term "privacy" which applies to so many things valued in Western society, is hardly to be found in the Chinese language!

Familial Individualism. All this seems to be the very antithesis of individualism. Yet, on the other hand, Chinese society was in some ways intensely individualistic. The key to this seeming paradox lies in identifying correctly the "individual." In Chinese traditional culture the "individual" was not the person, it was the family. Thus we find in China a form of *familial individualism*. Perhaps as a natural concomitant of the lack of personal individualism, familial individualism in China is intense, perhaps even extreme. Since the family group was so charged with responsibility for the behavior of its members, its unity tended to be very tight. Personal individualism of course suffers from the weakness that no person can truly live to himself. But familial individualism enjoys the privileges (and penalties) of individualism, while also gaining for the members making up the family the advantages of group support and strength. Family individualism is thus flexible. The family is a surer and more stable single entity than any one person can possibly be, and its survival value is far higher. At the same time, the family unit is a sharp competitive instrument, particularly when the various ages, temperaments, and abilities of the family members are welded into one keen weapon against the opposition.

This kind of thing could naturally grow up and survive in a wide agricultural countryside not susceptible to too much control from any central governmental authority. The best way to govern in this environment was, indeed, to govern not too much. The towns and cities were the seats of the larger government, but here, too, society was organized around the family. Crafts and trades were organized into guilds and other associations, but these were local or, at most, provincial in their scope. The sense of locality was very keen, so much so that the imperial government carefully avoided the dispatch of any bureaucrat to work in his locality of origin, lest he be taken back immediately into the family or other local unit and thus lose his value as an agent of the central authority. In collecting taxes and preserving order for the imperial government he acted for the most part upon collective entities. These were the families, villages, guilds, and associations which taxed their members for their own purposes, including payment of their imposts to the higher authorities of general government.

Limits on Imperial Authority. Largely excluded, thus, from government operations were the regulatory functions characteristic of more integrated and less particularistic societies. Certain kinds of public works were, indeed, the primary responsibility of the central authority. Included were irrigation and flood control enterprises. But not all these by any means were initiated or maintained by the central government. Above all, the major problems of land utilization, production, and distribution were simply outside the control of the central government. Thus the people were free to expand their use of agricultural land to include areas which were unsuitable from the point of view of water supply, soil, terrain, or elevation, but where from time to time and with occasional favorable conditions a crop could be gathered. The use of such soil was a desperate gamble, forced upon the people by pressure of population upon the land. It produced alternating periods of famine and starvation for those unfortunate enough to be forced onto unfavorable areas of land. It also produced many evils for those who had good land. For example, when hillsides were cultivated, the trees and other vegetation were destroyed. As a result, the rainfall normally held in the soil by this vegetation ran off instead into the streams. Thus rivers were flooded and the fertile valleys ruined for cultivation for greater or lesser periods. Disaster fell upon all alike.

The denudation of hills and mountains has progressed through Chinese history until today there are no great areas of major forests left in the traditionally Chinese territory south of the Great Wall. The cutting of the forests was not solely the result of pressure for more farm land; it went far beyond that. The wood was used for construction and for fuel and its use was essentially uncontrolled by agencies of government. This accentuated the problems of water control which gave rise to so much of the human misery seen throughout Chinese history. The imperial government, try as it might, could never keep fully abreast of these problems. Its work in building dams and dykes for flood prevention and irrigation merely accentuated its problems by increasing the production of foodstuffs in local areas. This, in turn, seemed inevitably to mean an increase in the population, with resultant expansion of cultivation to marginal areas. This would, in turn, bring on an entire new cycle of water conservancy problems to a government unable to interfere in any way at the source of it all. In truth, the greater the peace and prosperity of the countryside, the more certainly did there develop sooner or later an imbalance between population and agricultural resources.

Imperial Responsibility and the "Right of Revolution." When this type of situation became general throughout the country, the full paradox of Chinese imperial government became evident. The government, claiming absolute obedience in those fields which it did control, could also be held responsible for matters which it could not very well have controlled even if it had desired to. This situation was aggravated by the political theory under which the Emperor was considered the religious intermediary between the people and the world they lived in, on the one hand, and the mysterious and unseen spiritual world. Natural disasters on any great scale were considered signs that the Emperor had lost the approval of "Heaven" and had thus lost his "mandate" to rule over the people. Under such circumstances, the theory ran, the people had the right of revolution. But any such revolution, to overthrow the Imperial House, was treason, and subjected its supporters to summary execution.

Thus the right of revolution, stated in the writings of the philosopher Mencius who lived in China in the fourth and third centuries B.C., was a right which could only be asserted at great personal risk. Even to discuss rebellion was an act of treason. This meant that overt action against the central government was likely to await the accumulation of grievances so heavy and widespread as to make a try at rebellion inevitable, even if it were to fail. Rebellions were thus preceded by long periods of hidden conspiracy to which the close organization of the family, clan, and association were admirably adapted. In fact, conspiracy was almost the only form of political action open to the ordinary person, at least as far as the central government was concerned. And conspiracy placed a burden upon one's friends, a burden so heavy that friendship could hardly be considered a casual matter. Either friends were "all for" each other, or they were hardly friends at all. In China today, friendship is still an "all or nothing" relationship, the basis for enterprise and profit, not easily entered into, and not likely to be abandoned for any reason of a purely legal and formal nature.

When finally the power of the Imperial House to suppress rebellion was weakened by the accumulation of its difficulties on all sides, and when its inability to conduct the normal business of government had resulted in political chaos, then some new and fresh rebellion would succeed. The imperial family would be extirpated and a new claimant of the "Mandate of Heaven" would seat himself on the throne. In the process of all this there would be a heavy loss of life. The peasantry, its numbers greatly thinned out by war, pestilence, and famine, would readjust itself gradually to the agricultural environment in such a way that the balance between population and food supply would be restored. And, after sometimes very long periods of war and disorder, a new time of peace and prosperity would come. Every such epoch carried with it the seeds of its own destruction: a growing population forcing agricultural production in the marginal lands beyond the limits of real profit. Thus a new cycle of growth and decay in Chinese society would begin.

Western Contacts to 1842. The pretensions of the imperial government of China to absolutism within the country were paralleled externally by a belief in the universality of China. All non-Chinese were simply regarded as barbarians. Those in the regions surrounding China were held under varying degrees of military control when China was strong enough to do so. At other times they were treated as satellite areas. Thus, areas as remote from each other as Korea on the northeast, and Tibet and Burma in the west and southwest, were from time to time held in a relationship to which there is no exact parallel in Western international law. The aim of China was to allow them local self-government but to control fully their relations with other countries. In addition, these countries were to be provided with the advantages of Chinese culture and learning, and were to some extent tied to the Empire with trade. The complete superiority of China to these satellite states was unquestioned, certainly in the mind of the Chinese themselves.

Early Western contacts with China were considered by the Chinese court merely as new episodes in the long history of troubles with the barbarians. In their early contacts with China by sea, western Europeans confirmed this notion. Early navigators to the East acted indeed like piratical raiders. They would seize local points along the coasts of south Asian countries and use them as trading posts or as starting points for penetration of the interior. The dividing line between trade and piracy was rather thin. The fact that these foreigners brought their religion with them did nothing to improve the reputation of either the Westerners themselves or their religion.

When these people moved along the coast of south and southeast Asia and reached China, they followed the same system. The Portuguese claimed Macao after 1557 and used it as a trading post. But the Chinese were not much interested in trade with the Westerners. Chinese material civilization was so superior to that of western Europe that the Europeans had little or nothing to offer for the greatly superior products produced by Chinese agriculture and handicraft. Silk, cotton cloth, porcelain, and tea were all greatly desired.

Christianity also had come into China in early times but had not made much impact on the self-satisfied Chinese. However, when Christian missionaries began to emphasize Western scientific learning, such as astronomy, mathematics, and geography, they began to win a measure of acceptance. In time they threw this advantage away, by arguing among themselves as to the relation between Christianity and the indigenous Confucian cult centering upon ancestor-worship. When this dispute was decided by the Pope, the Chinese Emperor considered it an incursion on his universal authority over his subjects, and in 1724 banned Christianity from his domain. In 1757 also, trade was strictly limited as to where it could be carried on.

The Westerners submitted; they could do nothing else. They wanted the trade badly enough to agree, and felt unable to challenge the Chinese power. In 1793 and again in 1816, the British sent official missions to China to secure better conditions, but the Chinese summarily rejected these efforts. They treated the emissaries as tribute-bearers and regarded Britain as just another subject satellite state, however distant it might be. (*See Reading No. 1.*)

Meanwhile, the trade grew. By 1729 the foreign traders were importing opium to China and thus began to solve the problem of payment for Chinese goods. The trade in this commodity grew slowly, as production was gradually increased in areas like northeastern India. Between 1796 and 1839 the amounts imported into China increased by some thirty times, setting up an outflow of silver currency from China to pay for it, and thus creating serious economic problems for the Empire. The trade in opium had always been illegal, but neither Chinese officials nor Western traders had paid much attention to this. But the government of China was finally forced to do something about the outflow of silver money, and strict prohibition of the opium trade resulted.

The Opium War. This led finally to war. British investment in the production and sale of opium was sufficiently important to have brought about hostilities. This motive was greatly reinforced by the desire to end, once and for all, the to them unsatisfactory conditions of relations with China. In view of the history of Western imperialism in south and southeastern Asia, the Chinese had ample reason for their policy of exclusion against Western trade and religion. They were determined to keep the intruders in their place by a policy of "unequal treatment." The Westerners, on their part were determined to achieve recognition as equals, to break the Chinese system of isolating them in small areas of residence and work at Canton, and to open up the large Chinese hinterland to their trade. In view of the long history of the illegal opium trade, they considered its summary and unilateral prohibition as unreasonable and arbitrary. But seldom in history has any war had a worse cause than did the war of 1839-1842, which has become known as the Opium War. It ended in a complete victory for the British.

In the meantime, the Russians had not been idle in the

north. By the middle of the seventeenth century they had penetrated east and south in Siberia to the Chinese border in the region of northeast Manchuria. They were also pushing against the Chinese boundaries in outer Mongolia and Turkestan. In a series of treaties the Chinese and Russians stabilized their trading and diplomatic relations and at least partially adjusted their long common frontier. In all this the Russians were treated by the Chinese as just another barbarian element, in this case an element strong enough so that the Chinese court had to compromise with it, temporarily it was hoped. In the process, the Russians painlessly extracted from the Chinese large segments of territory in the so-called Maritime Provinces to the northeast of present-day Manchuria. On this basis the relations between China and Russia were stabilized until the middle of the nineteenth century.

The Opening of China. After the Opium War a number of treaties were made between foreign powers and China. The British made two treaties, in 1842 and 1844. (*See Reading No. 2.*) The French and American treaties were concluded in 1844. By these agreements the Chinese undertook to open five ports on the southeast China coast, to the foreign trade. They agreed to establish in the areas set aside for foreign residence in these ports a measure of extraterritoriality under which jurisdiction over foreigners was to be in the hands of the foreign consular authorities and not in the hands of Chinese officials. They consented to the renewal of Christian missionary work in China. And above all, they agreed to conduct their relations with the foreign powers on a basis of international equality.

In these treaties the various countries inserted what is known as the "most-favored-nation clause," under which each power secured from the Chinese government a guarantee that in the future it would be treated as well as the most-favored-nation. This meant that any future concession secured from China by any one power would automatically be available to all other powers equally: in effect, that as the powers proceeded together in the opening up of China and the exploitation of the ensuing privileges, no one power would gain an undue advantage over the others. This made it possible for countries like the

United States, which did not engage in these early wars against China, to secure for themselves all the concessions forced out of China by military action taken by others.

It was not long before further trouble arose. The Chinese were determined to resist any genuine change in their relations with the foreigners. They were masters at delay and obstruction. Negotiations regarding differences in the interpretation of the treaties got nowhere. Two more wars followed, with England and France in 1856-1858 and the same powers 1859-1860. There were numerous new treaties and agreements, by which some of the remaining vestiges of the unequal treatment of foreign nations by China were abolished. For example, China's foreign relations were no longer to be conducted by the Bureau of Dependencies, but by a new Ministry of Foreign Affairs. On the other side, the foreigners expanded their own system of inequality in their own favor, by increasing the area of consular jurisdiction over their citizens residing in China. Access to the interior of China was greatly increased for both trade and missionary work. And large indemnities were imposed on China by the victorious powers. By joint action of China, Britain, and the United States, the trade in opium was fully legalized.

China's Internal Difficulties.   All this pressure by the foreign powers was naturally highly damaging to the power and prestige of the imperial government. Since 1644 the ruling dynasty had been a foreign one, the Ch'ing or Manchu dynasty. It had become thoroughly Chinese, and under its most eminent emperors China had enjoyed some periods of great material prosperity and cultural flowering. But by the middle of the nineteenth century the country had again reached a time of major internal crisis. Between 1786 and 1839 numerous rebellions had taken place, involving secret conspiracies, religious uprisings (Mohammedans) and wars by non-Chinese tribesmen. Much bloodshed and property destruction ensued. The inability of the dynasty to resist foreign aggression after 1839 was doubtless partly caused by the weakening effects of these rebellions upon the economy and upon the military establishment.

Following the first defeat by Britain, 1839-1842, and continuing through nearly thirty years, China was further convulsed by a series of very large rebellions, widely scattered throughout the empire. During this time there were at least six major rebellions, the average duration of which was nearly fourteen years! They were scattered widely through the country, including the south and central part, the north central, northwest, southwest and central Asia. All were put down, but at fantastic cost in life and property. One of these alone, the T'ai P'ing rebellion which lasted from 1848 to 1865, is calculated to have cost the lives of twenty million Chinese by fire, sword, pestilence, or starvation.

Much of the prosperous central China area was devastated, with results still visible eighty years later! Loyal Chinese scholar-statesmen were largely responsible for putting down these rebellions and saving the dynasty, but the ruling house seemed completely unable to draw the obvious moral from the situation. Its capacity to mobilize any great resistance to Western aggression was severely curtailed, but this did not prevent the court from spending large sums on inconsequential luxuries. The notorious Empress Dowager T'zu Hsi in fact appropriated twenty million ounces of silver intended for use in building a navy and spent it on a palace garden! Yet the dynasty hung on for fifty years, in spite of everything. It was a man made of straw, but no one quite dared to push it over. How many millions had already gone to their death in the attempt!

China and the Powers, 1860-1894. The attitude of the foreigners toward the rebellions and other internal difficulties of China was a mixed one. They would not have relished having a new government in Peking strong enough to take quick and decisive remedial measures. Such a government would also be strong enough to resist the pressure of foreign powers. By this time, the position of foreigners in China was dependent upon the concessions exacted from the Peking government through war, negotiation, and pressure, and thus the foreign powers had a stake in the continued existence of the Manchu regime. As a result they were generally anti-rebel, and actually gave some help to the imperial government against rebels, especially those in areas where their own trading and residence rights might be endangered by a rebel success. Such help as they gave was never decisive in putting down any rebellion, but it showed the

attitude of the powers clearly. Would a strong and recon-
structed China be in their interest? Despite some statements to this effect they actually feared a strong China
more than a weak one.

This dilemma has always confronted those who have
sought to exploit the Chinese people in modern times,
and it has been basically insoluble. Foreign influences
upon China could hardly help but strengthen it, even if
slowly and imperceptibly. How could this be reconciled
with getting out of China what they wanted?

Between 1860 and 1875 the powers generally coöperated in a policy of ending Chinese seclusion and the exclusion of foreigners. They had, for example, never succeeded in getting for their diplomats in China the right
of audience with the Emperor. On this point the Chinese
resisted as long as they could, and when they finally
granted an audience, held it in the hall where tributary
missions from the vassal states were customarily received.
The Chinese also refrained from sending resident missions abroad. None was sent until 1877, when representatives were sent to England. On matters such as this the
powers acted in unison for a time, but after 1875 their
coöperation broke down and it was everyone for himself.

Chinese relations with the foreigners inside China were
also very difficult. The Chinese attitude was generally one
of hostility. That of the foreigners was one of arrogance.
The vast cultural gulf between them, their mutual ignorance of each other, made both Chinese and foreigners, for
differing reasons, look down upon and despise each other.
There was an element of mutual fear also. The Chinese
feared the cultural and economic activity of the foreigners
as a threat to their age-old civilization, which it unques-
tionably was. The Westerners were busily importing into
China their ideas and their religions which were entirely
incompatible with those of China. At the same time, their
economic activity, particularly in its technological aspects
such as communication and transport, threatened to dis-
integrate still further the traditional economic organization of a country already suffering from the gravest internal disorders.

The foreigners also feared the Chinese, at the same
time as they looked down on them for the most part. The

Westerners were few, in a land of millions. They were there solely by reason of having forced their way in, and this was not calculated to make them trust their unwilling hosts. Hence, their armed force was constantly in the background, and indeed even their negotiations with the government became known as "gunboat diplomacy."

At the same time as they were thus by very mixed means trying to advance their position inside China, some of the powers were also eating away at the frontier territories of the Empire. The Russians, after a long period in which the frontier had been stabilized, began to bite off chunks of Chinese territory along the northeastern frontier. In 1886 the British, after a long series of related events, finally destroyed China's claim to suzerainty over northern Burma. And the French who had been pressing to gain control in the region of Indo-China since 1858 finally destroyed China's nominal control over Tongkong and Annam in 1884-1885 and began to push against the southwestern provinces of China itself. In 1881 Japan gained control over the Liu Ch'iu (Ryukyu) islands after a long struggle to destroy China's hold there.

Emigration Problems. One of the most difficult problems in Chinese relations with the outside world was that of emigration. Migration from China had long been prohibited by the imperial government, but the rule was not enforced. In connection with the opening up of China after 1844 the Chinese government worked for the right of its emigrants overseas to enjoy full equality with migrants from other nations. (*See Reading No. 3.*) By 1867 there were in California alone already some 50,000 Chinese who were a welcome source of cheap labor in the early days of gold mining and railway construction. In July 1868 the United States formally agreed to allow Chinese the right to enter the country and be treated on an equal basis with immigrants from other countries. But when, within the next fifteen years, the number of Chinese laborers in California multiplied over two and one-half times, local opposition became strong. Local restrictions were enacted, and the Chinese suffered various forms of ill-treatment. In response to pressure in this country the treaty with China was revised and Congress soon shut off all entry of Chinese for ten years. But the ill-treatment continued. When the reports reached China, the impact of this upon the treatment of United States citizens there can easily be imagined.

Chinese immigrants to South American countries suffered far more than those in the United States. They were shipped out of south China under conditions like those of the slave trade, and when they reached their destination they were treated worse than slaves. Most of this so-called "contract labor" came out of the Portuguese port of Macao in south China, and after 1875, under pressure from the British, the Portuguese gradually brought this infamous traffic to an end. But great damage was done to Chinese-foreign relations by mistreatment of Chinese nationals abroad, and particularly by the refusal of nations like the United States to live up to their treaty obligations in this respect, when at the same time they were pushing hard for the fulfillment of treaties by the Chinese government. (*See Reading No. 4.*)

The Missionary Movement in China. Much of the impact of troubles between the Chinese and foreign governments was felt immediately by Christian missionaries in China. Both Catholic and Nestorian missionaries had reached China as early as 1300, but had little permanent impact. In the sixteenth and seventeenth centuries a renewed missionary movement brought such eminent Catholics as Matthew Ricci to live and work in China. The proscription of Christianity in 1724 caused a decline in the spread of the religion, but it is estimated that by 1800 there were some 200,000 Catholic Chinese. Protestant missionaries did not reach China until 1807.

After the opening of the interior of China to foreigners about 1860 the numbers of missionaries increased greatly and they soon were working in every chinese province. During the hundred years from 1800 to 1900 the number of Chinese Catholics increased to 500,000 and there were a total of about 55,000 Chinese Protestants. The missionaries brought not only their religion but their educational system. They were largely responsible for the beginnings of modern medicine in China.

Western religion and culture was thus striking hard at the basics of Chinese civilization. An example of its destructiveness can be seen in the opposition of missionaries to such practices as ancestor-worship. The worship of ancestors had been a component of Chinese life, and the religious cornerstone of family unity, since before 1500 B.C. When the missionaries told the Chinese that to become Christians it was necessary to give up this practice, they were truly striking at the root of the one institution, the family, which had always been the focus of loyalty and the center of activity for the Chinese. To expect this sort of attack to go unchallenged in public and official opinion would be to expect the impossible. Good, orthodox Chinese, raised in the traditions of the centuries, were outraged by such ideas. In addition, there is no doubt but that Christianity brought with it certain abuses. Missionaries and their work were supported from abroad, with foreign money. Converts shared this support, and in some cases it was the chief reason for their acceptance of Christianity. In addition, in view of the opposition of the rank and file to Christianity and the violence which such opposition sometimes aroused, the converts had from time to time to be protected or backed up by the threat of foreign military power.

As a result of this general situation, many disorders arose. There were persecutions, riots, and massacres of Chinese and foreign Christians. The foreign powers made a point of demanding full protection for missionary work, but the Chinese government often could not, and sometimes would not, provide it. The government at Peking tried, in fact, to secure control of the missionaries through treaty revision, but the powers would never consent to this.

Educational, Cultural, and Psychological Developments. For the missionaries, some degree of mastery of the Chinese language was essential to the propagation of their religion to the people. Their study of the language led to the compilation of dictionaries, and to the translation of Chinese classical and literary works into Western languages. It also led to the translation of considerable quantities of Western material into Chinese, and not all of this, by any means, was religious in subject matter. The missionary schools, started first at the primary level, and later going on to more advanced education, began to give a very few Chinese a knowledge of the outside world. In 1872 the Chinese government sent its first educational mission to the outside world, as a result of which some

120 young Chinese students had some education in the
United States. By official opposition this project was
abruptly halted less than ten years after it began, however.
In 1865 a school established in Peking to supply foreign-
language interpreters to the government was expanded
into a college, teaching scientific subjects in addition to
languages.

All this was firmly opposed by the vast majority of the
Chinese scholarly and bureaucratic elite. The impact of
these measures on the masses was of course infinitesimal,
but these activities might have been greatly increased at
the time, with correspondingly quicker and more general
results, if it had not been for the extreme opposition of the
Chinese literate elite. In searching for the reasons for this
we may come to understand some of the most basic problems of modern China.

These problems have their root in the mentality of the
educated minority. It was this minority of scholar-bureaucrats that exercised the power on behalf of the ruling
house. We have already stated that they entered office by
passing civil service examinations stressing memorization
of the classics and mastery of literary style. They were by
no means technically educated, nor were they specialists
in the use of violence and force. How could such people
control a country? The answer is, of course, that they did
not. The country ran itself, for the most part on the
village level, while these functionaries stood by to col-
lect the taxes and see to it that public tranquility was
preserved. Their ability to read and write made them
good keepers of the records, but it also gave them command of the general civic morality embedded in the classical writings. It was the primary responsibility of the educated minority to propagate this morality to the great mass
of the people. In a practical situation the quotation of
the relevant classical maxim was the formula for securing
action and making policy. This placed an emphasis upon
rote memorization and upon the subjective interpretation
of classics which, it was believed, had the power and
efficacy of scripture.

Thus, skill in the use of words, and reliance upon subjective mental processes, came to characterize the ruling
bureaucracy of China through the ages. When in the nineteenth century Western military force consistently de-

feated the best China could bring to bear against it, the bureaucrats and the court took refuge behind the impenetrable barriers of their own subjectivity. They were not much impressed by Western arms even when their superiority was objectively demonstrated on the field of battle. They had never been trained, for the most part, in the business of relating material implementation to the support of ideas and values. This sort of thing they left to the farmers, artisans, and traders, and sometimes, to professional soldiers. This latter class had been largely absent from, or in a very weak position in, Chinese society since the destruction of Chinese feudalism two hundred years before Christ. The rebellions and the successful revolutions were led by amateurs turned soldier, and they were opposed, at least in the nineteenth century, by scholar-bureaucrats at the head of great levies of raw peasant manpower armed for the most part with crude weapons derived from and associated with farm implements.

This pattern of war-making had always sufficed before, but it could not suffice against gunpowder and naval vessels. The few professional soldiers available to the Manchu court were the hereditary descendants of garrisons planted upon China in the seventeenth century at the time the Manchus took over the country.

Thus it was that during the latter part of the nineteenth century the Chinese incurred defeat after defeat at the hands of the West while preserving almost untouched the myth of their own superiority and the assurance of their own adequacy. The sheer massiveness of Chinese self-assurance at that time, after more than fifty years of being hammered about the ears by Western power, must surely be one of the most striking psychological and cultural phenomena of our times! Its tragic consequence was that China refused to change. At the same time its smaller and heretofore somewhat despised neighbor, Japan, was rapidly adopting Western techniques for the purpose of protecting its traditional way of life. For Japan this meant the construction of modern military power, and this in turn necessitated modern industry. In the search for security the Japanese therefore turned to foreign conquest. They sought for geographical barriers to possible aggression and for the sources of the materials they

needed for industry. In view of China's weakness she was
the logical objective for Japan to attack. This attack
opened up an entirely new phase of China's modern
history.

— 2 —

REFORM, REVOLUTION, AND RECONSTRUCTION, 1895-1930

China and Japan Struggle over Korea. Since the
fifteenth century, Korea had been a vassal of China. Her
internal government and general international affairs were
her own business, provided always that she acknowledged
China's overlordship. In return for this, China was obli-
gated to help in any defense of Korea against foreign
attack. In the nineteenth century Korea was at a low
point in her national history, with her ruling house largely
ineffectual and her administration riddled by factionalism.

Japanese pressure on Korea in modern times was
rooted in economics and military strategy. The rice of
Korea was important to the growing population of Japan.
And the possibility existed that an expanding Russia might
control the Korean peninsula and from it threaten Japan.
In 1876 Korea and Japan signed a treaty which the
Japanese interpreted to mean that Korea was a fully
sovereign and independent state. Both China and Japan
tried to play politics among the factions in Korean government, with the result that both powers brought troops
into Korea. When fighting broke out between them, both
subsequently agreed to withdraw. But later when anti-
foreign disorders became general, the government requested China's help. The Japanese also sent their troops
in. War began between China and Japan.

The First Sino-Japanese War, 1894-1895. Japan's

rather quick and easy victory in the war with China came as a surprise to many who were deceived by China's sheer size, the mass of her manpower, etc. Japan's forces were small, but they were well equipped and trained, and led by professionally trained officers. By contrast, China's forces were divided up among local governors and were poorly equipped. The money which should have been spent on new armament had gone largely into the pockets of the corrupt officials. The Japanese navy first eliminated the Chinese fleet from the contest. The army then invaded Korea in force, and went on into Manchuria. Chinese resistance collapsed.

The Treaty of Shimonoseki (1895) ended the war. Southeast Manchuria was ceded to Japan, but Russia, France, and Germany intervened to force Japan to give it up. She did secure from China the island of Taiwan (Formosa) and neighboring islands. And, above all, the "independence and autonomy" of Korea were acknowledged by China. From then on control of Korea would be a matter strictly between Japan and Russia.

The Battle for Concessions in China, 1895-1898. The imperialist powers of the West were not long in drawing the appropriate moral from China's defeat. If China was so weak, the only logical course was for each power to grab its share and thus prevent anyone from achieving a complete monopoly. In this competition, Russia enjoyed some initial advantage because of its part in preventing Japan's takeover of southeast Manchuria after the war. Her bill for this service was quickly presented to China, and included economic and military-strategic penetration of Manchuria, clearly portending complete Russian domination. In 1896 Russia and China signed a treaty of alliance against Japan. Between 1897 and 1899 Russia secured from China a lease of the Liaotung Peninsula of south Manchuria, including the ports of Port Arthur and Dairen and a number of mining and railroad concessions.

The other powers were not idle. France in 1895 secured from China important economic and railroad rights, and a leasehold, in southwest China. As a result of the murder in 1897 by Chinese of two German missionaries, Germany in the following year secured a ninety-nine year leasehold in Shantung province, accompanied by economic concessions and privileges in that province. Britain's interest in China remained primarily commercial. Thus she viewed with alarm the trend toward partition of China. But she went along with others by securing a lease of the northern port of Weihaiwai for as long as Russia held Port Arthur, and also took a ninety-nine year lease on part of the Chinese mainland just opposite to her island colony of Hongkong. She also gained numerous important contracts for railroad building in China. The system of extraterritorial foreign concessions at the treaty ports was expanded. France, Germany, Russia, Japan, and Belgium all developed new concessions at this time.

Development of "Spheres of Interest" in China, 1898. All this made it seem as though China as a nation was about to disappear. This alarmed those powers with large stakes in commerce with China as a whole. England, France, and Japan accordingly moved to prevent the cession to any other power of those regions of China in which their trade was developing. In 1898 Britain secured from China a pledge that she would never give away to any other power any of the six provinces bordering on the Yangtze River. Soon thereafter France secured a similar pledge relating to three southern provinces, and to Hainan island off the south China coast. Japan secured the same guarantee regarding the coastal province of Fukien. Thus ten of the eighteen provinces south of the Great Wall were included in the so-called "spheres of interest" of these powers. Added to this was the already established German sphere in Shantung, and the Russian preserve in the three provinces of Manchuria. If China were to break up entirely, much of its richest territory had thus been pre-empted by these powers.

The Reform Movement, First Stage, 1898. Clearly, China's age-old technique of "playing one barbarian off against another" had entirely failed her. The Western imperialists were advancing together against China. China's defeat by Japan was a severe shock to many Chinese intellectuals who were now for the first time beginning to advocate reform. Perhaps the most prominent of these were Chang Chih-tung (1837-1909), K'ang Yu-wei (1858-1927), and Sun Yat-sen (1866-1925). These three men differed greatly in their ideas. Chang Chih-tung was a complete defender of the imperial dynasty and of Confucianism which he termed "our holy teaching." To protect the Chinese people and their nation from destruction, he would support the ancient moral order through the material strength derived from knowledge of modern ways and means. (*See Reading No. 5.*) He was a highly successful government official and administrator, and a practical advocate of modernization himself. If there had been enough others like him China's modernization might have developed from their work in the provinces they governed. But perhaps it was too late. How much self-regeneration of the political regime of China would be required before this could be done?

K'ang Yu-wei was among those few who saw this issue. He was not a practicing official like Chang, but a historian and philologist. His study of Confucianism led him to the conclusion that its ideas were being perverted by the monarchy and its obedient scholar-bureaucrat supporters. To him, Confucianism meant public spiritedness and equality instead of the corrupt selfishness and subjective authoritarianism then so current in governing circles. Constitutional monarchy would have been the end result, politically, of his thinking. Under the impact of the defeat by Japan, the Emperor agreed to K'ang's program for changing the civil service examinations to cover modern knowledge, taught in a reformed system of education.

The vast majority of the traditional scholar-bureaucrats strongly resisted these changes. When K'ang attempted to begin military and naval reforms he found that national control of the military hardly existed. His attempts to bring it about soon caught him up in court intrigue. He was denounced to the Empress Dowager, the real power behind the throne, who moved immediately to arrest the Emperor. K'ang barely escaped from China with his life, and spent the rest of his days working among the Chinese abroad.

Unlike Chang and K'ang, Sun Yat-sen was not educated in traditional Chinese learning, but took a degree in modern medicine, in Hongkong. He lived much of his life abroad, and in a sense was the only true revolutionary of the three. Unlike Chang and K'ang, Sun had had contact with many Western ideas, and it is no discredit to him to say that he could never really absorb them or work them into systematic form. Nationalism, democracy, socialism, all influenced him. In addition, he was a Christian. And above all, for most of his life he was a working revolutionary, dedicated to the overthrow of the Manchu dynasty and the substitution for it of a parliamentary form of government. He realized that for a long period the Chinese people would have to undergo "tutelage" to prepare them for self-government. Whence would come this "tutelage"? Could those leaders who themselves were haltingly groping for political solutions provide political tutelage for the masses?

The Boxer Movement, 1900.   The Empress Dowager did not stop with arresting the Emperor and driving out reformers. She also sanctioned a movement widely established in the militia forces and secret societies in North China, which came to be known as the Boxer Movement. Members of the Boxers were sworn to drive all foreigners out of China by force. The defeat of China by Japan, and the aggressive moves of foreign powers against China, were enough to produce wholesale anti-foreign disorders even if the Empress Dowager had not sanctioned them. In these disorders, more than two hundred missionaries and other foreigners were killed in north China, and thousands of Chineses converts also lost their lives. In many localities the high officials risked their own lives by refusing to join in the movement. Thus many foreigners were able to escape.

What would the foreign powers do to the imperial government of China? Would they bring it down in disgrace and help set up another? Or would they merely impose punishment? They chose the latter course. A huge indemnity was imposed. Numerous officials were punished, some with death. Foreign garrisons were permanently quartered in Peking and for policing communications between that city and the sea. Many other penalties were added. The United States had taken the lead in urging the restoration of the monarchy to power. For this she perhaps made partial recompense by remitting her part of the Boxer Indemnity and using it to set up a fund for Chinese education.

The Open Door Policy, 1899.   In the general scramble for concessions and spheres of influence in China following the first Sino-Japanese War, the attitude of Britain was based solidly upon her world-wide supremacy in commerce. She always felt able to win in commercial competition with anyone, anywhere in the world. Thus, Britain wanted the preservation of China's political entity, and open access for all to her trade.

The attitude of the United States had always been similar. We were against the creation of more European colonies in Asia, as we had been in Latin America. This was based partly upon political and ideological factors, and partly upon commercial hopes and expectations.

Thus neither Britain nor the United States wanted to see the so-called "spheres of influence" turned into genuine colonial possessions of the various powers. Accordingly, they renewed their coöperation, and with some British initiative, the United States, in September 1899, issued a series of notes to the various powers having "spheres of influence" in China. (*See Reading No. 6.*) In these notes the powers were asked to state that they would not monopolize trade in their spheres, but would instead preserve an "Open Door" for the trade of all nations. Equal and impartial trade for all, in all spheres of influence, would tend to prevent colonial-type commercial monopoly from fastening itself upon various parts of China, and would, in the process, at least slow down somewhat the rapid erosion of China's administrative and territorial integrity.

At the same time, however, the United States was embarking on her own course of colonial expansion in the Far East. During the Spanish-American War an American fleet had defeated the Spanish naval force in the Philippines. As a result, the United States annexed the islands in 1898 and 1899. As international rivalries then stood, it was unlikely that the islands could stand independent by themselves. They were likely to be taken by someone else if the United States cast them adrift. In the hands of the United States they could be used as a base from which to make American power felt in the Far East, in the interest of the most-favored-nation treatment for commerce, and of the policy of the Open Door and the territorial and administrative integrity of China. Such are the contradictions of foreign policy induced by the realities of power in foreign affairs.

The Russo-Japanese Struggle over Korea and Man-

churia, 1900-1905.   After the Japanese defeated China
in 1895, they began to prepare for the inevitable show-
down with Russia. They built up their army and navy. In
this struggle they took advantage of the international
situation. In the Far East, any southward movement by
Russia would provide ice-free ports for the Russian navy,
and thus tend to threaten Britain's naval defense in depth
of her vast holdings in Southeast Asia and India. The
United States and Japan joined Britain in the effort to
loosen the ever-tightening grip of Russia on Manchuria.
Even Germany joined in.

British policy in the Far East had always taken account
of the possibility that to head off the Russian southward
advance, direct military action might be called for. Accordingly, she had tried to help both China and Japan
build up their naval strength. But when Japan defeated
China so easily, it became clear that China could not be
counted on against Russia. In addition, since France was
an ally of Russia, Britain needed an ally against Russia
also, and particularly in the Far East. Accordingly, the
Anglo-Japanese Alliance was formed in 1902, under
which the two powers pledged their support to peace and
the existing territorial "status quo" in the Far East, and
specifically to the independence of China and Korea.
Britain's interests in China and Japan's in Korea were
mutually recognized, and the provision was made that if
either power went to war to defend these interests, the
other would be neutral. In case a third power intervened
in the war, then Britain or Japan would go to each other's
assistance.

Since Japan was unable to head off Russian advances in
Korea which threatened to take that country over, war
finally came in 1904. It was a naked struggle between
Russia and Japan for control of helpless Korea. The war
was fought in Korea, Manchuria, and on the sea, and
Japan won, again largely by opposing the vastly greater
potential of her enemy with smaller but better armed and
better led forces of her own. If the Russians, who at war's
end, were only beginning to rally much strength, particularly in their land forces, had hung on and struck back,
the Japanese could not have held out. Consequently,
since most of the powers sympathized with Japan, an intervention was arranged.

Under the terms of the Treaty of Portsmouth, 1905, Japan was again prevented from taking over the entire Russian position in Manchuria, though she did so in South Manchuria. But she secured complete domination in Korea, and within a few years completely absorbed that country into the Japanese Empire. This, and the Japanese takeover in South Manchuria were a rather stiff price to pay for the extinction once and for all, it was hoped, of the Russian threat to China. From then on Japan would bear the most watching as a threat to China.

New Efforts at Reform in China, 1901-1908. The Empress Dowager, Tz'u Hsi, had broken up the Emperor's attempt to adopt K'ang Yu-wei's reform program in 1898. But in the following year she launched a reform program of her own. But all her efforts ran up against the entrenched personal and local interests of the scholar-bureaucrats in the provinces. The more convinced they became of the weakness and eventual disintegration of the dynasty, the less they could be interested in measures to strengthen the dynasty.

In 1908 the Empress Dowager went so far as to announce a nine-year program of constitutional reform. But she merely attempted to write into a constitution the age-old Chinese system of imperial supremacy, while at the same time materially expanding the powers of the central government. Although they could not openly advocate any such thing, the radicals were holding out for the complete abolition of the monarchy. The entire country was honeycombed with revolutionary conspiracy. At any rate, the death of the Empress Dowager and the Emperor in 1908 ended these ineffective gestures at reform. P'u Yi, a child of three years, took over the throne.

Foreign Finance and China's Autonomy, 1900-1914. At the same time as these feeble and partial efforts were being made to strengthen China internally, the diplomacy of the foreign powers was threatening to enmesh China in a net of financial commitments, including foreign control of taxation and finance. Thus the Chinese government was being weakened by these measures of financial imperialism, at the very moment when it was attempting to take into its hands the control of finances largely dominated by the provincial administrations. Furthermore, the various powers tended to concentrate their financial investments in China in their several spheres of interest and particularly in and around their concessions in the port cities. This led to an unbalanced development in China, and particularly since the foreign banks tended to draw off free private capital from the Chinese countryside into the concessions, where it was immune from control or taxation by the Chinese government.

American participation in the financial game in China was rather sporadic. Early efforts at railroad development in Manchuria were unsuccessful. The Chinese government tried, as usual, to play the various bidders off against each other, but the foreign powers coöperated just enough to prevent any real competition in the market for financial loans in China. When the First World War began in 1914, the European powers were forced to withdraw, and this left Japan in a dominant financial position just at the time when the power of the Chinese to resist had fallen to a new low level after the Revolution of 1911.

The very immediate causes of the Revolution, indeed included the dissatisfaction in the provinces over the national government's attempt to centralize control of foreign railway financing, instead of leaving it in the hands of provincial administrators and business interests.

The Revolutionary Movement in China, 1895-1912 The successive failures to reform the Chinese government left the revolutionaries the only future source of political action. There were many revolutionaries both in and outside of China. Their main source of support was the Chinese who lived abroad, and all groups competed for this support. Chief organizer and agitator was Dr. Sun Yat-sen who, as early as 1894, organized a small revolutionary group in Hawaii with a branch organization in Japan. In 1905 he organized in Tokyo the Chung Kuo T'ung Meng Hui (Chinese Covenant Society), and later developed branches of this organization in Europe. The platform of this society contained three fundamentals: oust the Manchus and restore China to Chinese control; create a republic; and "distribute the land equally." Although all the various revolutionary groups were nationalistic and insisted on restoring the government of China to the Chinese, Sun's emphasis upon republicanism and land redistribution was his own idea. These three principles were later developed into the San Min Chu-i (Three People's Principles) of Sun Yat-sen and became the basis of the ideology of the Kuomintang (The Nationalist Party).

For such overseas organizations there was growing, though secret, support in China among the intellectuals who were taking in foreign ideas through the new education. Those who came back after being educated abroad, the so-called "returned students," were particularly infected with revolutionary ideas. In many cases their foreign education had made them culturally alien to almost everyone in China except the few others who had shared their experiences. Yet, perforce, they had to become the leaders of the coming revolution. It is not surprising that many of them found it easier rather indiscriminately to destroy the heritage of the past than to build firmly the future.

Overthrow of the Manchus and Establishment of the Republic, 1911-1912. There were numerous minor or abortive uprisings in central China and in the south and southwest parts of the country in 1904, 1906, 1907, 1908, and 1911. On October 10, 1911, an accidental bomb explosion in the city of Hankow, in central China, disclosed a revolutionary group, the members of which were executed. The next day, imperial troops in the area mutinied, under their leader a Col. Li Yuan-hung, and disaffection spread quickly to most of the imperial troops in the Yangtze River valley. On December 12, the city of Nanking was captured by the rebels, and a truce and Peace Conference between the rebels and the imperial government resulted.

On December 24, 1911, Dr. Sun Yat-sen arrived in Shanghai, and took office as President of a Provisional Government, with Li Yuan-hung, now a General in command of all the revolutionary troops, as Vice-President. The Imperial Court had tried during November to stave off complete disaster by promulgating a new constitution providing for a parliamentary, representative form of government, but it was too late. Negotiations, carried out by Dr. Sun and General Yuan Shih-kai, resulted on February 12, 1912, in the abdication of the Manchus who had held power in China since 1644. This also brought to an end the system of imperial government in China which had existed continuously since the third century B.C.

The Presidency of Yuan Shih-kai, 1912-1916. Yuan Shih-kai (1859-1916) had long been a devoted and honored servant of the Manchu dynasty. In December 1911, he had been made Premier, and in the last days of the Imperial House he gained complete control over the court. He was, thus, the one man with whom the revolutionaries under Dr. Sun had to negotiate for the abdication, and it soon became apparent that he was handling things so as to succeed to power when the Manchus were eliminated. The revolutionaries were willing to make him President of their new Republic. But after his assumption of office as Provisional President on February 15, 1912, it soon became obvious that he was still a monarchist and that he intended nothing less than the establishment of a new dynasty with himself as the first Emperor. A little more than a year after the Manchu abdication, Dr. Sun and his Kuomintang opened a revolt against Yuan Shih-kai. This rebellion failed, and Sun and the others had to flee the country. Yuan ruled as a dictator from then on, and in 1915 a "convention" was held in Peking which invited him to take over the throne. After a due amount of ceremonial hesitation, he consented.

At this point, the foreign powers, who had recognized Yuan as President all along, took alarm. The anti-monarchists rebelled in the southwest in 1915, and in March 1916, Yuan Shih-kai canceled the monarchy and promised a responsible Cabinet which would control the Executive. But his resignation was insisted upon, and when he refused, a number of provinces in central, southern, and southwestern China withdrew their support from the government and set up their own regimes. Yuan died that same year and was succeeded by Li Yuan-hung who had been Vice-President under him.

International Relations of China, 1911-1926. Korea was not the only tributary region over which the Chinese lost their suzerainty in the waning days of the Empire. Tibet was increasingly influenced and controlled by Britain. Outer Mongolia came more and more under Russian influence and finally became "autonomous" from China and went under complete Russian domination.

When war began in Europe in 1914, China would have benefitted from neutrality and noninvolvement. But this was not to be. Japan joined the Allies and attacked the German leasehold at Kiaochow Bay (Tsingtao), in Shantung Province, in 1914. She violated Chinese soil in this action. In January 1915, Japan forwarded to the Chinese government in Peking the so-called Twenty-one Demands, which aimed at making China a protectorate of Japan. The European powers were too much occupied with the war to interfere. They needed Japanese naval support against Germany and were quite prepared to sell out China to Japan if necessary to get it. The United States, however, notified Japan that she would not recognize any infringement by Japan upon her treaty rights in China. Here was an actual precedent for the Stimson policy of nonrecognition as applied to Japan's Manchurian aggression some seventeen years later.

In August 1917, partly because of American pressure, China entered the European war. This caused great internal dissension in China, and a number of provinces rebelled. Japanese influence remained strong in Peking. The United States tried to prevent this from developing into another threat of Japanese takeover, and in the process an agreement with Japan, the Lansing-Ishii Agreement, 1917, was formulated. In this Agreement, both Japan and the United States stated their adherence to the Open Door Policy for China, but the United States recognized that Japan "has special interests in China, particularly in the part to which her possessions are contiguous." This began to sound a little too much like Japan's previous assertion of her "paramount interests" in Korea, the achievement of which had resulted in nothing less than the extinction of Korea as a state. When, at the Peace Conference, Japan was confirmed in her possession of the former German holding in Shantung, a wave of nationalism and anti-foreignism swept China.

By entry into the European War China recovered all the former Austro-Hungarian and German concessions outside of Shantung, and in her separate treaty of peace the Central Powers gave up the rights of extraterritoriality. This provision was inserted also in all treaties with the new states of Europe that emerged from the war. And she became a member of the League of Nations, where eventually she was to protest Japan's later aggression against her, in Manchuria.

With the end of the war, and the Peace Conference, the basic opposition was clear between the traditional Anglo-American policy of the Open Door and support of China's administrative and territorial integrity, and the rather obvious aims of Japan to nullify this policy. United States–Japanese tensions arising out of this situation were sufficiently strong to help lead toward a race in naval armaments. The United States could have outbuilt Japan with relative ease, but for reasons of pacifism and economy, the American public strongly opposed an armaments race.

At the Washington Conference of 1921-1922, the Japanese were compelled to accept a ratio of three capital ships (battleships) to five each for the American and British navies. But they gained supposed immunity from attack by either Britain or the United States through the agreement that neither of these powers could construct naval bases in the northwest Pacific. Under the terms of the Nine-Power treaty, all those powers with interests in China (except the Soviet Union which was not present at Washington) agreed to respect China's sovereignty and territorial integrity, to support equal trade opportunities for all in China, and to refrain from all attempts to secure special privileges in respect to China which would abridge the rights or privileges of citizens of friendly states there. For the first time, the Open Door Policy had been embodied in a general international agreement. (*See Reading No. 7.*)

But the Japanese, who returned their Shantung holdings to China and abandoned the worst of the Twenty-one Demands upon China, could now build up effective naval supremacy in the western Pacific, behind which they could feel free later to abandon the pledges they were forced into at Washington. Failure of Britain and the United States to build up to the authorized limits in capital ships helped to convince the Japanese that they would be immune from American reprisal in case they renewed their aggressive policy toward China. Here was a situation with explosive potentialities for the future!

Internal Confusion and Warlordism in China, 1916-1926. During this period the powers recognized a series of "governments" in Peking, but the real power was in the hands of local leaders, the "warlords" of the period. Some of these were former imperial officials. Others had come up from the peasantry, or were bandits who by violence had consolidated their rule over vast areas of suffering China. Always their aims were to win out over all rivals for power and to support claims to rule over all China.

There was nothing new in this basic pattern. Many times in the past when dynasties had fallen, long periods of disorder had followed in which contesting claimants to the supreme power had fought it out among themselves. Sometimes a period of fifty or one hundred years had passed before China was again unified under a single regime. In the meantime, smaller warlords built themselves into greater ones. The struggle hit the common man hard, with tax levies and conscription for the armies. But, by and large, the struggle between the rivals for supreme power seemed of no direct interest to the people, who only wished it "would go away and leave us alone." There were some moves toward federation among the various warlords, but in general the prospects for national unification seemed very dim.

The Kuomintang and Chinese Nationalism, 1917-1926.   In all this chaos and anarchy Dr. Sun Yat-sen and his Kuomintang seemed to get nowhere. Sun was a devoted revolutionary, and he had developed a number of constructive ideas for China's future, but he could not set up or maintain for long any practical administration of government. His party was beset with petty factionalism, the curse of Chinese politics in modern times. If Sun had been merely a crude military man, perhaps he might have been able to deal harshly with the undisciplined, but instead he fell victim to a succession of intriguers for power within his own group. He could not secure help from the Western powers. He could never build any military force which would serve the purpose of his party. In fact, it is doubtful whether he ever really understood the relation between military power and his revolutionary political objectives.

In January 1923, after one of his periods of removal from South China where the Kuomintang carried on its precarious existence, Dr. Sun returned to Canton. Be-

tween 1923 and 1926 a series of changes took place in
his party, which carried it finally to success.

Some of Dr. Sun's early doctrines were beginning to
take on new meaning as time went by. (*See Reading
No. 8.*) The doctrine of "socialism or people's livelihood," became attractive to a number of the younger
radicals, largely because it could be claimed to be successfully current in the U.S.S.R. In addition, the rising
tide of anti-foreignism in China during and after the First
World War gave new meaning to Dr. Sun's doctrines of
"nationalism" which he had originally aimed at the Manchu dynasty. Communist agents of the Soviet Union and
their sympathizers in China worked hard to turn Chinese
anti-foreignism and national feeling into pro-Communism,
and with considerable success. Anything Russian had a
high prestige with the Kuomintang and its followers because, having failed to get support from the Western
powers in spite of willingness to make concessions to
them, Dr. Sun turned to the ready and waiting Russians
and did secure material assistance from that source. Chinese Communists, in considerable numbers, joined the
Kuomintang. They brought to it the powerful discipline
characteristic of their party, something very much needed
in the Kuomintang, faction-ridden as it always had been.

But none of this might have availed without one other
essential ingredient. This was provided by the action of
Dr. Sun in sending to the Soviet Union in 1924 a young
Kuomintang member and military officer, Chiang Kai-
shek. Born in the province of Chekiang in 1887, Chiang
Kai-shek had been educated in military academies in
China and Japan and had joined the revolutionary movement while in Japan. He had participated in the 1911
revolution. In 1923 he was Chief of Staff in the Headquarters of the Commander in Chief of the Kuomintang
forces. His mission to the Soviet Union lasted four
months, during which time he seemed most impressed by
the tight organization and discipline of the Russian Communists. He came back to recommend that the Kuomintang and the armed forces supporting it be reorganized
under strong, disciplined central control.

In May 1924, the Whampoa Military Academy was
established to train officers to lead the Kuomintang forces,
and Chiang Kai-shek was placed in charge. Cadets were

carefully chosen and were given stiff military training, accompanied by political education. Army leadership improved, so that by 1926 the two chief southern provinces of Kwangtung and Kwangsi were both solidly under Kuomintang control, with armed forces of about 90,000 men.

When Dr. Sun died in Peking on March 12, 1925, while negotiating with the regime there, the administration of which he had been head was abolished and a Nationalist Government was set up on July 1. The Nationalists, as they will be termed from here on, were getting stronger.

The Nationalist Takeover of China, 1926-1930. By 1926 the factions in the Nationalist party and government had been reduced to the number of two. These were the Communists on one side and the non-Communist and anti-Communist original party members on the other. Chiang Kai-shek headed the anti-Communist group. He took action to free the army from Communist influence by sending the Russian military advisors back to the U.S.S.R. But he avoided a complete break with the pro-Communist elements in the party and government. In June 1926, he was placed in command of the Nationalist army, and within two years he had crushed all the warlords in the north who refused to come over to the Nationalists. The allegiance of some of those who came over was rather weak, to say the least, and a number were left in effective control of their local areas just so long as they professed allegiance to the Nationalist government which by this time had set up its national capital in Nanking.

The Communist elements remained a threat. In 1927, they set up a separate government in Hankow, and from there controlled the province of Hunan. But Chiang Kai-shek struck hard against them, with the financial backing of the business interests of Shanghai. The Communists were driven into the countryside in south-central China where a continued war raged between them and the forces of Chiang Kai-shek.

In Nationalist-controlled China it was a time of prosperity. Chiang Kai-shek headed the administration, and under his leadership the government balanced its budget and won the support of foreign governments by a sound program of national consolidation. Much progress was made toward the abolition of special foreign privileges in China and the regaining of full rights of internal self-government. This brought friction from two sources, the U.S.S.R. and Japan. The troubles with the U.S.S.R. arose from Chinese efforts to regain full powers of government in Manchuria. But these were rather transitory. The U.S.S.R. did not wish a general embroilment with China, especially over matters of "rights recovery" which she had long advocated for China and continued to advocate as long, of course, as the recovery rights by China did not threaten too severely any of the special privileges of the U.S.S.R. itself.

Japan, on the other hand, became most apprehensive lest the rising nationalism of China under Chiang Kai-shek should threaten all her "special interests," in China, and particularly in Manchuria. Direct conflict between Chinese nationalism and Japanese imperialism had to come, and it did, in 1931.

Economic and Social Developments, 1895-1930. During the thirty-five years before 1930, the struggle to create a new Chinese national government had been essentially political and military, but it was conducted in an economic and social environment which was highly disturbed, to say the least. How could there be established the necessary economic support for the continued military effort to establish unity? Chiang Kai-shek's answer to this was simple and effective. When his capital was established in Nanking, he gained control of the Yangtze valley area, the most prosperous area of the nation. The tax revenues from the trade and commerce of this area were devoted to the support of his war against the Communists. This was costly, but since both sides were limited as to weapons and equipment which they could secure from China's limited resources, the slight edge in modern weapons which Chiang Kai-shek could gain from his superior financial power provided him with an important advantage.

The Nationalist struggle to regain the foreign concession areas was at least partially a struggle for the control of money and finance in China. War and chaos in China had driven capital into these concessions. The Nationalists could not take them by force. Anti-foreign violence had occurred during the Nationalist advance to the north from Canton, as in Nanking in 1927. And it had shown the likelihood that to direct attacks on the foreign concessions would invite violent foreign reaction. In the process no one could gain: all would lose by destruction of the properties built up in the concessions. Thus compromise was called for on both sides, and the result was that the Nationalists could tax the increasing profits to business which resulted from the increasing order and stability in the Yangtze river region. With this income it could purchase from abroad the airplanes, light tanks, automotive equipment, petroleum products, and heavier guns and ammunition which could not be manufactured in China. This, and the assistance of foreign military experts from abroad, chiefly from Germany and the United States, gave the Nationalist armies the power slowly to grind down the opposition forces, chiefly those of the Communists in south-central China.

China itself remained primarily an agricultural country. The Chinese people could survive many years of continuous civil war because of two facts. First, the armies and weapons of war which were being used in China generally lacked enough mass and power to bring general destruction to the productive facilities of any given area; and second, since there was no national economy, economic disruptions were chiefly local or regional and thus could not bring about a general economic crisis.

The country was kept economically divided by lack of modern communications. Railroad development was very slight except in Manchuria, an area dominated by Russia and Japan and where these powers developed railways under their own control. The use of the automobile and airplane was just beginning in China. Thus, trade between different major regions in China was a mere trickle. And China's foreign trade was a very slight part of total world trade. The early trade exporting tea, silk and cotton textiles, and porcelains, for furs, specie, and opium had long since died out. The industrialized Western countries exported cheap cotton cloth to China, and this killed off most of the handicraft weaving in China. The mechanized textile industry had gotten started in China, mostly in the foreign concessions like Shanghai, where Chinese cotton and cheap labor were combined with imported machinery to produce cloth still cheaper than the imported product. The new imports also included petroleum products (chiefly kerosene for lamps), tobacco, machinery and automotive equipment, and raw cotton. Food imports climbed, for the most part sugar and wheat. And for these imports China traded her agricultural products, such as vegetable oils, eggs, and pig bristles, together with some minerals such as tungsten, tin, and antimony.

By 1931 the United States had taken first place in this trade, supplanting Britain, and with Japan a close second. Britain's capital investment in China was still by far the largest of the foreign powers, and her position in finance, insurance, and shipping was dominant. Yet there was a growing tendency for the Chinese to adopt Western models in trade and finance, and to deal directly with producers abroad.

For a century, wars and revolutions had been commonplace. But the eighty or eighty-five per cent of China's people who gained their living directly from the soil could still survive. During the century before 1931, the total population doubtless increased, in spite of wars, famines, and pestilences. The result has been a steady decrease in agricultural land per person and constant pressure upon the individual farmer. This led to an increase of landlordism, since the farmers in many places were driven by economic pressure to go to the moneylender and place their land under mortgage at such high rates of interest that they never could repay their loans and would therefore lose their land. In an age of such general personal and economic insecurity, interest rates and rents were bound to remain high. All this, together with extortionate taxation by local regimes, particularly in the warlord period, put the farmer in a perpetual squeeze.

During all this time, economic localism was paralleled by the traditional family-centered and locality-centered psychology and social organization of the Chinese. This was as it had always been before. Changes in the tenure of national power from dynasty to dynasty had never been accompanied by revolutionary disturbances in the society as a whole. But now, for the first time, the external pressures on China were arousing resistance far below the surface.

It was no accident, therefore, that the government of Chiang Kai-shek which now gave China its best administration in a century, was known as the Nationalist Government. It gained support from the trading nations, Britain and the United States, who, it was thought, could be depended upon to move with it in the direction of a truly self-governing China. At this point, China, Britain, and the United States parted company from Japan. They were later to become common allies in a war against Japanese imperialism.

Cultural and Ideological Developments in China, to 1930. Political disruption in China was paralleled by disintegration in its intellectual and cultural life. For the most part, the great mass of the people were not immediately affected, but China had never been ruled by the masses. What of the elite, the educated ten per cent, who enjoyed power in China far, far out of proportion to their numbers?

Among these people, there was general intellectual chaos. The old ideas had been largely abandoned, and imported non-Chinese ideas competed to fill the vacuum. As the growing numbers of Chinese students went abroad, ranging over America, Europe, Japan, and the U.S.S.R. they came back to China with every conceivable type of viewpoint. They had a tendency, perhaps inherited from their Confucian background, to ally themselves with particular "schools" of thought. These were of all kinds, including Christianity, anarchism, Western science as a cure-all, socialism, internationalism, free capitalism, rational anti-religionism, and republican democracy. Of course, many of these ideas were exotically foreign to the Chinese, but some intellectuals spent a great deal of time offering proofs that some of these things had been known to the Chinese tradition long ago, hoping thus to make them more acceptable to their contemporaries.

All this intellectual interplay demonstrated the remarkable facility, capacity for learning, and energy, of the minds of the Chinese intellectuals. The liberation at this time of so much sheer mental energy was not surprising when we remember that the abandonment of the old tradition meant to the younger intellectuals freedom from a set of ideas, Confucianism, which, unfortunately, had become highly stereotyped and conventionalized in interpretation and application.

But their new freedom was often a too-intoxicating wine for the intellectuals, many of whom failed to understand that in gaining their freedom they had also begun to lose their monopoly of power. They no longer had any secure road to rulership, although many did enter government service after taking academic degrees at home or (mostly) abroad. They never did play a determining role in reconstituting order in the nation. But here again they were following tradition, since always, with dynastic shifts of power, the scholar bureaucrats had waited for the reestablishment of order by the cruder military means, and then proceeded to offer their services to the newly incumbent regimes.

Some few of the rising intellectuals saw, indeed, that to follow Western democratic ideas would require them to abdicate their monopoly of power. Some therefore prepared to abandon the elitism of their class, characteristic of the previous centuries of scholar-bureaucratic rule under the Empire. They began to prepare for general mass participation in the cultural, governmental, and political activities of the country. First steps were taken to decrease the gap between the rather remote intellectual world of the scholar-elite and the minds of the people. Here was a problem of the greatest magnitude. Scholars, for example, had been trained in a highly formalized classical written language which they used only to communicate with each other. Dr. Sun Yat-sen, for example, wrote his revolutionary manifestoes in this language. And at the other end of the political scale, probably ninety per cent of the people could not read at all!

The movement to abandon the classical written language and write only in the vernacular spoken style (*pai hua*), was headed by Dr. Hu Shih (born 1891) who had been educated in the United States. (*See Reading No. 9.*) With the rapid progress of this movement, a great many periodicals soon sprang up, and *pai hua* soon became the common medium of literary, scientific, and journalistic communication.

But the great task of making all this available to the masses depended upon eliminating the general illiteracy.

This was a herculean task. Even in 1938, twenty-six years after the Revolution of 1912, the National Government estimated the total number of illiterate persons in China at 360,000,000, more than twice the total population of the United States today! This figure was some eighty-six per cent of China's population at the time. Even today, if only an estimated seventy per cent of a possible population of 600,000,000 on the Chinese mainland are illiterate, there would be 60,000,000 more illiterate persons in China in 1959 than twenty-one years previously in 1938! Such are the fundamental problems against which the abstract ideologies of government must be tested.

Perhaps the greatest single ideological innovation of the Chinese Revolution has been the idea of nationalism, Chinese nationalism vis-à-vis the outside world. Yet this ideology was not, for the most part, implanted in China by intellectuals, ideologues, or educators. Chinese nationalism was evoked, elicited, and created among Chinese at all levels of intellect and education, only by a century of foreign aggression against China. Dr. Sun Yat-sen and his followers had propagandized for nationalism for years among the Chinese intellectuals without much success.

But when Chiang Kai-shek, a military specialist educated in China and Japan, put behind this idea the power of a tightly organized and small but effective army, he was organizing support behind an idea which spontaneous Chinese demonstrations had already shown to be appealing. Thus the regime to which Dr. Sun had long before given the name Nationalist, succeeded as no other revolutionary regime had up to then, in attainment of national power and successful government.

Perhaps the moral of this is that in thinking of the modern Chinese revolution we should pay less attention to the intellectual warfare and the "isms" *as such,* and more to the success or failure of implementing these "isms" in programs of action. Above all, the success or failure of "isms" is very often a function of military success or failure. Another moral we may draw is that many, if not most, of the important *internal* developments in modern China are heavily dependent upon external influences. What, for instance, was to be the reaction of the still-burgeoning Japanese imperialism to the newly rising Chinese nationalism and to the National Government which was so actively fostering and building it?

— 3 —

WAR AND ITS AFTERMATH, 1931-1949

Japan in Manchuria, 1905-1931. For a quarter-century after taking over the Russian position in South Manchuria, Japan invested great efforts and much capital in the economic development of the area, particularly heavy industry, mining, power production, and rail and river transportation. The rail system of South Manchuria connected directly with that of North China, and over these lines after 1911 had poured into Manchuria the millions of Chinese farmers who fled North China's famines and floods. Thus in 1931 the population of Manchuria was about ninety-eight per cent Chinese. Japan never succeeded in sending very many of her own people there, despite crowded conditions at home. But Japanese business administrators and professional men and military found important work there. South Manchuria became a virtual commercial monopoly of Japan, and Manchurian heavy industry, notably the steel plants, became vital to Japan's economic and military modernization. Agricultural production increased steadily as new land was opened by the Chinese farmers, and crops of Manchuria became important in world and regional trade.

Japanese Aggression in Manchuria, 1931-1933. The combined military and economic position of Japan in Manchuria led during the years to a virtual extinction of Chinese control there. However, Chinese warlordism developed in Manchuria in the rule of the ex-bandit Chang Tso-lin, who ruled parts of the country outside. the

Japanese-held zones and railway areas. After the Nationalists came to power in China, their drive to recover all foreign-held rights in China directly threatened the now vital interests which Japan had built up in Manchuria at so much expense. The Chinese government began to build railways in Manchuria outside the Japanese leased areas in South Manchuria. Since these lines in many cases paralleled Japanese lines, they constituted an obvious declaration of war by China against the Japanese monopoly of business in Manchuria. Other difficulties arose over Japanese protection of Korean farmers in Manchuria, as well as over Japanese espionage activities in Manchuria. Although these problems were under constant negotiation between the foreign offices of China and Japan, the Japanese military decided on direct action to drive the Chinese Government and its forces out of Manchuria once and for all.

Consequently the Japanese army in Manchuria, in clear defiance of higher Japanese authority both civil and military, manufactured a spurious "incident" on September 18, 1931, in which, they claimed, the Chinese had bombed the railway near Mukden. They went on to take over all Manchuria. To this action the United States reacted with what has since become known as the "Stimson Doctrine," that the United States would not recognize the legality of any *de facto* situation, or of any agreement, which would impair its rights in China or run counter to the Open Door Policy. (*See Reading No. 10.*)

After the Japanese attacked at Shanghai on January 28, 1932, to break up a severe Chinese boycott of Japanese goods and to intimidate China, the League of Nations Assembly on March 11, 1932, unanimously disapproved Japan's actions both in Manchuria and Shanghai. But in Manchuria Japan set up the puppet state of "Manchukuo" to include the three Manchurian provinces and the North China province of Jehol. Japan recognized this puppet state on September 15. When the League of Nations condemned her actions in Manchuria and urged retention of Chinese sovereignty there, Japan gave notice on March 27, 1933, of her intention to withdraw from that body. The League could not control Japan. Its failure to halt Japanese aggression against China foreshadowed the doom

of the entire post-World War I system of collective
security.

Communist Russia and China's Border Territories.
After its defeat by Japan in 1905 Russia had held on
in Northern Manchuria. But after Japan had extinguished
Chinese control in Manchuria after 1931, the Russians
gradually liquidated their position there in favor of the
Japanese. In Mongolia, however, it was another story.
While still recognizing Chinese sovereignty over Outer
Mongolia the Soviets had in fact established there a pup-
pet government of their own, the so-called "Mongol
Peoples' Republic." Russia's major concern was to erect
a military-strategic buffer directly south of the central
part of the trans-Siberian Railroad.

Directly west and southwest of Outer Mongolia lay the
Chinese territory of Sinkiang or Chinese Turkestan bordering directly on Asiatic Russia. The Soviets also penetrated it. But they have never controlled it as consistently
as they have controlled Outer Mongolia.

Japan and Mongolia, 1931-1939. Numerous armed
clashes developed after 1931 along the long frontier between "Manchukuo," Siberia, and Outer Mongolia. Perhaps the largest was the battle fought in the Manchurian-
Outer Mongolian frontier region of Nomonhan, on May
11, 1939, when the Japanese were heavily defeated by
Russian and Mongol mechanized forces under General
Voroshilov. Long before this time Japan had tried to
subvert the Mongols of southwestern Manchuria and use
them to penetrate Inner Mongolia in North China, but to
no avail. Her war with China which began in 1937 included an attack through Inner Mongolia which brought
her to the southern frontiers of the Soviet puppet state in
Outer Mongolia. But this strategy of simultaneous pressure on Outer Mongolia from Manchuria and North
China was ended by the German-Soviet Alliance of 1939
and the subsequent Soviet-Japanese nonaggression pact of
1941.

Japanese Pressures on North China, 1931-1937.
The ease with which they had taken Manchuria and Jehol
tempted the Japanese military leaders to absorb as much
as they could of China south of the Great Wall. Also,
there were plentiful supplies in North China of iron, coal,
cotton, and salt, all of which could well be used in Japan's

industries. This, and their strategy of pressure against the Soviet Union from northern China and Inner Mongolia, led the Japanese army straight into North China and on toward Peiping (Peking). When they approached that city, in May 1933, a truce was arranged under which the region was demilitarized, supposedly under Chinese administration. In the truce zone there was a complete Japanese economic takeover, including extensive smuggling of both ordinary trade goods and narcotics, and a linkage between the local currency and that of Japan.

The National Government under Chiang Kai-shek seemed powerless to resist. It was Chiang's strategy to hold off and to compromise in order to gain time to build up strength for eventual war with Japan. He knew he could not win now. But in this policy he was severely handicapped by rising popular anger with Japan and by the pressure for war from student organizations. Was Japan to take over all of China by stages? If so, how could China ever mobilize the strength to resist in the end? (*See Reading No. 11.*)

Internal Developments in China, 1931-1937. Despite simultaneous civil war and foreign invasion, the Nationalist Government at Nanking made very substantial progress. It pressed the foreign powers for complete recovery of its rights of internal self-government, including full control of customs administration and abolition of foreign extraterritorial rights on Chinese soil. The first of these two objectives was achieved in full. The end of all foreign leaseholds on Chinese soil was clearly only a matter of time, and the foreign concessions enjoying immunity from Chinese jurisdiction were slowly being closed out. This caused genuine alarm to those Japanese who planned complete domination of China.

At this time there was also considerable industrialization and construction of railroads and highways. The world-wide economic depression did not spare China. Because of monetary policies elsewhere over which the Chinese government had no control, the value of silver rose in terms of the Chinese currency and commodities. United States silver purchases drained out much specie from China. Both foreign and internal trade were handicapped by low prices for goods, and numerous business and financial failures decreased the revenues of the central government. This helped reinforce Chiang Kai-shek's policy of compromise with the Japanese over Manchuria and North China.

Civil War with the Communists, 1931-1937. The considerable diplomatic and economic successes of the Nationalist Government at this time should not blind us to the continuing lack of internal unity in China. Some progress was being made in the elimination or subordination to the National Government of the various local regimes in China. But the civil war between the Government and the Chinese Communists went on steadily through most of this time. The Communists at one time controlled more than 300,000 square miles of territory in south-central China in Kiangsi and contiguous provinces. Communist centers were chiefly in the mountains and rural areas. They could not survive in the cities, from which they had long since fled under pressure of government police. They had started as a movement of middle-class intellectuals and proletarians, but by the early 'thirties had been forced to the countryside. Here they worked to gain peasant support; but in order to do so they had to abandon for the time being their more doctrinaire Marxist ideas, such as that of state ownership of land.

The Chinese peasant has always had one central personal aim, namely to own land in his own right and enjoy for himself and his family the fruits of his labor. To gain support from the peasants, however temporary, the Chinese Communists at this time attacked the principle of private property in land only obliquely. They concentrated first on government *control* of private property in land, through regulating the amount of rent that could be charged to tenants. They also in some cases took land away from those who owned it and distributed it to nonowners. These landless peasants were happy to get land and were not much inclined to realize that such an indirect attack on the principle of private property in land might well be extended, at the proper time and place, to include *everyone's* property, even that of the small-holding peasant himself. Such, in fact, has been the subsequent history of Chinese Communist policy, so that today most peasants of Communist-held China are no longer allowed to own any land or other property.

Against the Communists the National Government

waged a ruthless war of extermination. By 1934, five successive campaigns had been launched against their areas in south-central China, and they were finally driven out and set forth on a long journey to northwest China, but only about 20,000 survivors arrived there. The National Government pressed the war against them, using for the most part the Manchurian troops who had fled to North China when the Japanese took their home provinces. They were not very enthusiastic about this war they were fighting so far from home, and were easily victimized by Communist subversive agents.

When Chiang Kai-shek went to northwest China in December 1936 to speed up the anti-Communist campaign, he was taken prisoner by some of these troops who demanded an end to the anti-Communist war and the beginning of military resistance to Japan. Chiang refused both these demands, and the Communists were all for killing him then and there. But they quickly received peremptory orders from the Comintern to release him. The Comintern knew that Wang Ching-wei, an arch-rival of Chiang Kai-shek in the Nationalist party, was on his way to Shanghai from Germay whence he had come with the blessing of Hitler. If he had taken over the Nationalist party, the Chinese government, already strongly influenced by the Germans, would have co-operated with the anti-Comintern powers, Germany and Japan, and with their help would have crushed the Chinese Communists forthwith, no doubt with Japanese assistance. This would have laid bare to Japanese pressures the whole Russian border with China, from the Yellow Sea to Turkestan. The only way for the Comintern to preserve the Chinese Communists was, oddly enough, to preserve Chiang Kai-shek at the same time!

By this time the pressures of the Japanese in North China were so severe that the Government in Nanking had to turn to resist them. This forced the virtual cessation of hostilities against the Communists, who were thus saved by Japan from certain extermination at the hands of the Government.

The Sino-Japanese War, 1937-1941. In Japan itself the military elements achieved increasing control over national policy. There was growing belief in the inevitability of Japan's control over all of China and in the consolidation of East Asia into a "Greater East Asia Co-prosperity Sphere" under Japanese domination. (*See Reading No. 12.*) The threat that under Chiang Kai-shek's leadership China might at last become unified and strong, led Japan to a forestalling policy. Her plan to take over the five North China provinces of Shansi, Suiyuan, Chahar, Hopei, and Shantung was not progressing well, and was likely to fare worse once the Communists and the Government stopped fighting each other in that region. The inevitable happened when the Japanese tried to take over a vital railway junction near Peiping on July 7, 1937, and Chinese resistance precipitated general war which was not to end until 1945.

War in North China quickly expanded. On August 13, 1937, Japan attacked at Shanghai. She was temporarily stopped by bitter Chinese resistance there but Nanking finally fell in December. The Government had evacuated to Hankow, some 400 miles up the river, and as the Japanese continued west the Government moved to Chungking, in far Szechwan Province. Japanese forces moved along the chief rivers and rail lines, but could never penetrate successfully west of the mountains except by aerial bombing, which could not break the Chinese will to fight. The Japanese tried to conquer all of China and to occupy it, but instead they merely tied down large forces to hold the chief lines of communication, and could not extend their control far into the countryside. Their naval blockade of the China coast was effective except for a minor loophole in Hongkong.

During the four and one-half years of the Sino-Japanese War before Pearl Harbor, the Japanese established puppet regimes in Inner Mongolia, in North China, and at Nanking in addition to the puppet regime of "Manchukuo." Added to this there was the Communist organization centered in the northwest, and the National Government of China at Chungking. Thus there were some six rival groups seeking total or regional power in China at that time. And this does not include a number of local war-lord remnant regimes in the northwest and south-west who ruled their areas with a large measure of autonomy while acknowledging allegiance to the National Government.

The Axis powers, Germany, Italy, and Japan, recog-

nized the Japanese puppet regimes in China. The rest of
the powers, including the U.S.S.R., for the most part
recognized the National Government at Chungking. By
the time of Pearl Harbor, the National Government had
been almost steadily at war with Japan for ten years and
had been engaged in civil war with the Chinese Communists for almost all of that time. It had suffered greatly
from the attrition of its morale and manpower. But
Chiang Kai-shek's will to resist never faltered. He refused several rather tempting offers from the Japanese to
make peace.

Nationalist-Communist Relations, 1937-1941. After
Chiang Kai-shek had returned to Nanking from his brief
captivity in Sian, the Communists offered the Government various minor political and military concessions in
return for an anti-Japanese United Front. The Government refused. It was forced to come to terms with the
Communists only after the Japanese began their all-out
war against China in the summer of 1937. In the following September, terms were agreed to under which the
Communists agreed to (1) fight for the Three People's
Principles of Sun Yat-sen; (2) give up armed rebellion,
red propaganda, and land confiscation; (3) abolish the
Soviet Chinese Communist government and introduce a
government based upon "political rights"; and (4) abolish
the name of the Red Army and reorganize it as a part of
the National Government forces. Even if these terms had
been carried out completely by the Communists, which
they never were, they would, in fact, have preserved the
two essential components of the Communist revolutionary
apparatus, namely the Chinese Communist Party (CCP)
and the Red Army under a new name.

In return for these "concessions" the CCP was elevated
to a position of influence in China which it had never
occupied at any time since the break with Chiang Kai-
shek in 1927-1928. Chou En-lai, the leading Communist
under Mao Tse-tung, was sent to Chungking as liaison
officer and was taken into the National Government.
Around him, in the very heart of the capital of the National Government, was formed an extensive Communist
agitation and propaganda apparatus which functioned in
the area controlled by the Government to carry out the
aim of subverting that Government, isolating it from

every possible supporting faction and element and at the same time persuading gullible foreigners in Free China and abroad that CCP was "progressive," "democratic," and the only reliable center of armed resistance to Japan.

Why did Chiang Kai-shek tolerate this situation? It must be remembered here that Japanese pressures in North China forced him to stop fighting the Communists, and that he had to do so or risk losing his supply of arms and material from the Soviet Union. This, small as it was, was his chief outside supply until it was cut off after the German attack on the U.S.S.R. in 1941. In order to stop fighting the CCP he had to have some concessions from them, even paper ones, or risk loss of support in his own party.

Having given the CCP unprecedented opportunities for subversive activity in Free China, the Government multiplied its own countersubversive activities, particularly its secret police apparatus, only to be accused by its enemies at home and abroad of complete suppression of the opposition. And this at the very time that the CCP was publishing every day its own newspaper in Chungking and spreading it in Free China and to the outside world! Its open opposition to the Government was so clear and obvious that finally in anticipation of a complete break in relations the CCP ordered all its activities in Government areas to go underground. The exception was the staff of its newspaper in Chungking which was ordered to carry on until the end and even to be taken prisoner by the Government if necessary. This would seem to embody the CCP's own estimate of the importance of this paper to its propaganda work in Free China and the world.

The withdrawal of the Government to the far west and the inability of the Japanese to occupy much more than the main lines of communication in the vast area empty of Government control provided a great opportunity for the Communists. Their well-organized guerrilla forces infiltrated these areas and set up local administrations, all this contrary to the terms of their agreement with the Government. Here they compromised between the landlords and peasants in order to get the support of both. The local administrations they set up were widely advertised as both democratic and representative, but in fact were tightly controlled by CCP minorities. Government efforts to compete in these areas and activities ran into the fact that the Government, which had lost the support of its allied commercial groups now in cities under Japanese control, had neither motivation nor skills necessary to powerful political mobilization of the rural masses. The support of the landlord groups in Free China was deemed vital to continuation of the Government there and to prosecution of the war. Thus insufficient importance was attached to direct competition with the Communists in the countryside, particularly in guerrilla warfare. Finally, the increasing expansion of the CCP by such means brought open rupture with the Government.

The United Front had received its death-blow in the West from the Nazi-Soviet nonaggression pact of 1939; so the Chinese Communists could abandon it without doing violence to the international Communist line. By January 1941, fighting broke out between Communists and Government forces, ending the United Front for good and all. Both sides were conserving their strength, actually, to fight it out after the defeat of Japan.

Internal Developments in Free China, 1937-1941. Several million people went with the Government when it migrated to western China, in 1937 and 1938. These included Government officials, businessmen, cultural leaders, and students. The officials and businessmen were largely concentrated in Chungking, with the latter group also represented in scattered areas throughout the West. The cultural leaders and students were heavily concentrated in cities and towns outside the capital, such as Kunming and Chengtu, but many of them stayed close to the capital. West China had up to then been relatively undeveloped economically and technically. It was largely unprepared to receive the migration of several millions of Chinese from the more advanced parts of East China. These migrants were therefore often forced to live and work under very adverse conditions, and on even less income than they were accustomed to before. Teachers and students in particular suffered from crowded and inadequate living conditions and from mounting inflation.

But in Chungking itself, where the Japanese concentrated their bombing attacks, the misery of life was endured, and the war efforts sustained by patriotism which was only the greater as Japan's offensives increased.

The hope of substantial aid from abroad to help China win through was never abandoned even in the worst times. President Chiang Kai-shek's own long-range strategy for resistance to Japan was based heavily upon the belief that Japanese aggression had an unlimited ambition, and that pursuit of the ambition to rule others would bring the Japanese into direct conflict, sooner or later, with the free countries of the West.

Was this a forlorn hope, nurtured solely in the mind of an isolated military leader, shut off in the far back-country of China? This was the time when the American people, whatever their sentimental support for China, recoiled in shock from President Roosevelt's suggestion that aggressors should be "quarantined." There were doubtless many Americans who agreed with the eminent professor of that time who was heard to say that the life of one American boy was worth more than all the four hundred million people of China! The vast majority of the American people were opposed to any war. They would never attack anyone else, and they could not believe anyone else would be so foolish, or wicked, as to attack them. And those very few who told them the truth, namely that a war between Japan and the United States was inevitable as things were going, were branded as fools at best, and at worst warmongers. President Chiang Kai-shek was one of the few who knew in advance what would happen. He could not bring it about. All he did was to continue steadfastly to resist Japanese aggression without compromise, and leave the rest to the Japanese. Events proved him right. (*See Reading No. 11.*)

The opening up of China's west after 1937 brought progress to that area, at whatever cost. The Government tried to develop the communications of the region, with roads, river transport, and air transport. Small, but vital parts of the industrial plant of eastern China were moved up the Yangtze River in pieces and rebuilt in the west. Raw material resources were explored. Small-scale manufacturing was promoted, including many coöperatives, for the supply of military and civilian goods. Agricultural production was promoted through expansion of credit to farmers. But war-engendered shortages, made more severe by the influx of military and civilians to west China and by the disruption of normal communications to the outside world, became more and more severe as time went on. Consequent price rises caused much suffering, escially as the Government tried to keep down wages and salaries in order to prevent the inflation from mounting even more rapidly. And demoralization among the people was promoted by the allied policy of defeating the Axis first as the main threat, and thus delaying the ultimate defeat of Japan.

The United States and China, 1941-1945. The initial attitude of the American people toward the war between China and Japan was a peculiar mixture of apathy, neutralism, and pacifism, on the one hand, and an inherently contradictory combination of sentimental devotion to the Chinese people and of desire to profit from the trade in oil and scrap iron to Japan, on the other hand. There were many who would condemn Japan's aggression against China, but few who would advocate direct action against it.

What changed all this? Essentially, the American people never changed their minds; they simply had their minds changed for them by the Japanese attack at Pearl Harbor. And that attack was made almost inevitable by the following factors:

1. The Japanese advanced into Southeast Asia to cut southwest China off from outside contact through northern Indo-China, and to take over French Indo-China after the collapse of France in Europe. This posed a strong threat to British and Dutch colonial holdings in that area.

2. Increasing commitment in the American government to the cause of the West in Europe led to open opposition to Japan's southward advance into and toward the colonies of the West in Southeast Asia.

3. When warnings to Japan to cease and desist from this southward advance failed to produce any results, the United States associated herself with the British and Dutch in an embargo on oil, scrap iron, and military supplies to Japan. And the United States froze Japan's credits in this country.

Thus the United States set itself on the road to war with Japan, in spite of an overwhelming revulsion against any such idea in the mind of the American people. The European conflict and that in the Far East were tied

together. The change in American policy in the spring of
1941 to one of direct opposition to Japan's war in Asia
began to show a few positive features by the following
summer, when a few political and military advisers were
sent to Free China. The shamefully low state of American
military preparedness at that time prevented any real help.
The Japanese, on their part, decided that they must take
the sources of oil in the Dutch colony of Indonesia and
that they should dispose of the American fleet at Pearl
Harbor first, before turning south. After the severe losses
suffered by the American fleet at Pearl Harbor, the
United States was even less able to help Free China than
before. Congress voted a $500,000,000 credit to China in
early 1942, but gold bars were a poor substitute for guns,
ammunition, gasoline, and airplanes.

Disappointment and frustration marked both sides in
Chinese-American relations for several years after Pearl
Harbor. The combined forces of the Chinese, Americans,
and British were defeated and driven out of Burma by the
Japanese. This cut the last land link of any importance
between Free China and the outside world. The Chinese
tried to get the United States to abandon or modify the
strategy of defeating Hitler and Mussolini first, but did
not succeed. The establishment of a slender aerial life-
line "over the Hump" to China from India was of great
symbolic importance to China, but it produced some of
the bitterest possible quarrels between the American
military in China as to who would get the small quantities
of freight it was thus possible to bring in. Finally, General
Stilwell, American commander in the area, brought on a
serious disagreement with President Chiang Kai-shek.
Stilwell, with the support of State Department representatives in China, proposed that Chinese Communist forces
be armed by the United States to fight the Japanese, as
a part of a unified Chinese armed force under his command. Chiang Kai-shek vetoed this proposal, even after
he was threatened by the United States and Britain with
removal of lendlease unless he complied.

On the positive side were the brilliant achievements of
American fliers in China in defending against Japanese
airpower, both before and after Pearl Harbor. The U.S.
Fourteenth Air Force in China under the command of

General Claire Chennault made a fine defensive and
offensive record, ranging as far as the Formosa Strait
and the South China Sea to harass Japanese shipping and
destroy Japanese air and land power. Northern Burma
was retaken from the Japanese and a road built from
India through its jungles to connect with the Burma road
into southwest China. A pipe line for petroleum products
was built parallel to it. This gave us a direct land connection into southwest China, a dubious advantage in view of
the great land area of China through which we would
have to fight in order to defeat Japan in China. It proved
quicker, if not easier, to fight back through the Pacific
toward Japan, than to go all the way across China and,
even then, find a broad expanse of water between us
and Japan.

In the meantime the United States and Britain had
taken the very important action in 1942 of unilaterally
renouncing for the future all their remaining special
privileges in China. This included all concessions, extraterritoriality, and all leaseholds except those of Britain in
Kowloon, the territory on the Chinese mainland immediately adjoining the Crown Colony of Hongkong. In
1943 the U.S. Congress repealed the Chinese Exclusion
Laws which had for so long been a barrier to good relations between America and China, as well as with Asia
in general.

**Internal Developments under the National Govern-
ment, 1941-1945.** As we have seen, Chinese hopes for
early help after the entry of the United States into the war
were doomed to disappointment. The successes of Japanese arms during the first six months after Pearl Harbor
were, in fact, greater than at any previous time since
1933. Within that time the Japanese evicted the Americans from the Philippines, and the British and Dutch
from Southeast Asia, in lightning campaigns which
demonstrated a superior mastery of jungle warfare, am-
phibious warfare, and of land-based and naval aviation.
Inside China, between 1941 and 1944, the Japanese
advanced with the object of producing Chinese surrender
before the United States could rally its forces and bring
help. As American submarine warfare cut heavily into
Japanese sea transport to and from Southeast Asia, a

further Japanese aim in China was to set up a land route joining Korea and Manchuria to South China and Southeast Asia, through Indo-China and Malaya.

By the end of 1944 most of this had been achieved. But still China held out. Chiang Kai-shek would not surrender.

Under these circumstances, as could well be expected, rapid deterioration beset Free China. The inflation, already serious, went out of control. It was caused by blockade, shortages of all kinds, inadequate production of all types of goods, and inability of the government to control prices, or wages except of bureaucrats and the military. It damaged all wage earners, but it demoralized the bureaucracy and the intellectuals, two groups upon whose support the Government was particularly dependent. Some price rises, in such areas as food, were due to Chinese supply of the increasing numbers of Americans, both civil and military, in China. There was a near-breakdown of road transport because of inability to get trucks and necessary fuel for them from abroad. The lack of transport affected seriously the supply of military forces. Inefficiencies in military administration were even more debilitating when accentuated by corrupt fiscal practices in the army, often forced upon officers and men by the inflation and the sometimes critical lack of supply. Requisitioning of supplies from the populace had sometimes to be resorted to, and this, together with the recruiting practices of the Nationalist Army, caused serious disaffection at times.

At the same time, there was altogether too much self-seeking in high quarters. Some officials of the central administration were in a position to make profits out of manipulating currency and commodities at a time of rapid inflation of prices. The age-old official practices, inherited from the past, of graft and peculation, were far from being rooted out, and at this time of sagging morale such practices were indulged in by high officials of the government. President Chiang Kai-shek was himself entirely blameless in this respect, but his dependence upon the support of a small clique of his long-time associates and relatives made them immune from the penalties they should have suffered for their misdemeanors.

All this added up to a growing political disunity in

Free China as the war went on. To the general exhaustion and the lack of Allied support there was added the conviction, by contrast, that the defeat of Japan was insured by Allied might, sooner or later. There was thus less call for the patriotic fervor which before Pearl Harbor had been such a unifying factor in Free China. Military weaknesses and official misconduct provided ample ammunition for political warfare, and open criticism of the government mounted. Dissident groups pressed for representative government. Some room for discussion was provided by the People's Political Council. Serving the purposes of a forum, it had no legislative function. In it a number of minor or incipient political groupings were represented. The Nationalist party (Kuomintang) monopolized the powers and responsibilities of government. Subversive activities were curbed by strict police methods, including secret police, the control and supervision of organizations of all types, concentration camps, and executions.

What was the attitude of the United States on these problems? Even before Pearl Harbor the attitude of personnel in the American Embassy in Chungking toward the Chinese Nationalists was one of open cynicism and disillusion. As conditions in Free China steadily worsened after 1941, Embassy officials pressed for reform of the Government. But they had little or no leverage upon it. They urged national unity and mobilization of all, including the Chinese Communists, in war upon the Japanese. But they had no way to supply the arms necessary for such a war. They pressed for liberalization of the Chinese government, but at a time when war pressures were forcing free governments everywhere in the opposite direction. They thus did much to create distrust of the United States in Chinese leadership, and fear and apprehension on the part of the Chinese government toward the United States. (*See Reading No. 13.*)

To many American officials concerned with Chinese affairs, "liberalization" of the Chinese government seemed to call for the admission of the Chinese Communists to a measure of governmental power. State Department personnel in China also backed General Stilwell's proposals for arming the Chinese Communists, which would have increased their military power in China. To both the

Communists and Nationalists these proposals necessarily involved the fundamental question of who would control China after the war was over.

The State Department's answer to this question was that control should be divided, or shared, in the general framework of a "Coalition Government." Both Communists and Nationalists were agreeable to a coalition, provided the outcome would be ultimate domination by their side, to be followed as soon as possible by liquidation of the other side. The Communists were willing to go in for political participation, provided they could retain independent control of their armed forces. They could thus hold out for political control within a coalition, or if unsuccessful in getting this, they could return to civil war. The Nationalists, on their side, made as a prerequisite to sharing of political power the integration of Communist armed forces into a national army under Government control. If they could achieve this, the Communists could not take over political domination by force, and the Nationalists could then liquidate them at their leisure. Seen in this light, the American government's official policy, urged by the State Department, of coalition between Communists and Nationalists, was utterly without foundation in reality. Whatever the compromise of the moment, coalition was genuinely unacceptable to both sides in the Chinese civil war.

The Growth of Chinese Communism, 1941-1945. By 1941 the United Front as a military factor had virtually collapsed. Politically, there were some remnants of it in the continued Chinese Communist propaganda activities in Government areas, and the contacts between Communists and the Government over the matter of coalition. Mao Tse-tung had provided ideological justification for the United Front in his *New Democracy,* but with the death of the United Front, the CCP instituted rigorous purges, in 1942 and 1943, to drive out those many newcomers who might have crept into the party under the United Front as "liberals" instead of hard-core Communists. These purges have always been supported and justified by the Communists under the principle that "politics" is really war, a war for the complete elimination and liquidation of the opposition. Hence, absolute military discipline in the organization is not only acceptable but necessary for self-preservation. The sacrifice of the individual and his freedom of thought or action is therefore the rule, not the exception.

Simultaneous with strict internal regimentation the Communists maintained their armed struggle with and against the non-Communists for the control of China. In the vast areas not under Japanese or Government control, the Communists took over control of local anti-Japanese guerrilla units, annihilating those which would not cooperate. They attacked Government forces, preferably after they had been fighting Japanese forces. Both arms and men were captured in this way. Survivors would either join the Communists or be liquidated. Subversive work was carried on inside Government forces to instigate defections. Local militia units were organized among the peasantry in areas where neither Japanese or Government control existed, and these units were absorbed by the Communists. By these methods the Communists greatly increased their armed forces.

Consequently, the Japanese in 1943 turned their attention to the Communists and defeated them with great losses. By 1945 the Communists had built up again, and by the end of the war their forces were entirely outside the control of the Government. The Government, on the other hand, had its forces built up by the end of the war with American training and equipment. Both sides looked forward to renewal of active civil war at the earliest possible moment. Both sides fundamentally rejected the basic American policy of substituting a political *modus vivendi* between them for the civil war which had continued almost unbroken for nearly twenty years.

During all this time Mao Tse-tung was building up a solid political machine in the CCP. He became the undisputed ideological authority of the CCP. In addition, the successive purges were used to eliminate all cliques hostile to him. An extensive use was made of positive ideological molding, to guarantee the united discipline of party members under Mao's leadership. This must be contrasted with the policy of Chiang Kai-shek in the Kuomintang, of tolerating cliques and playing them off one against the other to guarantee his own supremacy. This was a far less "efficient" approach, perhaps, to the problem of personal control. But what would his American friends, let alone

his enemies, have said if he had tried to establish in Free
China a monolithic party and governmental structure by
liquidation of the opposition on the model of Mao Tse-
tung?

The Postwar Planning for China, 1943-1945. Un-
real as was the official American policy of coalition
government to settle China's greatest internal problem,
its unreality was more than matched by our policy for
China in the international field. Here we set out to give
China the status of a "Great Power" in postwar affairs.
This was in spite of its economic backwardness, its military weaknesses, and its near-anarchy in internal politics.
It is hard to account for this. Perhaps it was merely the
natural direct continuation of our traditional China-
centered Far Eastern policy, characterized always by
hopefulness for the future of China. Perhaps it was based
on illusions of Chinese strength, caused by the sheer
length of China's rather lonely resistance to Japan, in
contrast to the rapidity with which the United States,
Britain, France, and Holland had lost all their Far Eastern possessions to the Japanese. Perhaps our *military*
neglect of China in the years after Pearl Harbor led to
overcompensation in the purely *political* field.

But whatever the reasons, there is no doubt today that
it was premature, to say the least, to make China one of
the "Big Four" in postwar planning. Both the U.S.S.R.
and Britain, for differing reasons, were most reluctant to
go along with the United States in this.

In October 1943, China was given Great Power status
as cosignatory of the Moscow Declaration that united
war would be waged against those Axis powers against
which each signatory was fighting. At Cairo in November
1943, President Chiang Kai-shek was present with President Roosevelt and Prime Minister Churchill and they
agreed that, after surrender, Japan would be cut back
territorially to her status of 1868 and that "all territories
Japan has stolen from the Chinese, such as Manchuria,
Formosa, and the Pescadores, shall be restored to the
Republic of China." To this end, the war would be continued until Japan surrendered unconditionally.

When Roosevelt and Churchill met with Stalin at the
Teheran Conference, November-December, 1943, Chiang
could not be there since Stalin urged that his presence

might weaken the USSR's neutrality with Japan. But he agreed to enter the war against Japan when Germany had been defeated, and he raised territorial demands in this connection which would necessarily involve the Chinese territories. In February 1945, at Yalta, Stalin made these desires more explicit. He had apprised the Allies previously through diplomatic channels of what his demands would be. In addition to the restoration of all Russian territories taken by Japan in the Russo-Japanese War, 1905, he demanded that the Soviet Union be restored to the Czarist pre-1905 position in the Chinese territory of Manchuria, and that "the status quo in Outer-Mongolia (The Mongolian People's Republic) shall be preserved." China was not present at this conference, but even in her absence, Roosevelt and Churchill promised Stalin that these demands would be fulfilled by the Chinese after Japan's surrender. In return, Stalin promised to help liberate China from Japan and to make a treaty of friendship and alliance with the "National Government of China."

Accordingly, in August 1945, the Sino-Soviet treaty was made at Moscow, embodying these provisions. In addition, the Chinese agreed to a plebiscite in Outer Mongolia regarding its independence from China, and Stalin agreed to give military and other aid to the National Government and to it alone. Russia denied any interest on its part in Sinkiang and acknowledged full Chinese sovereignty over Manchuria. In view of its re-establishment there in full possession of the Czarist former position and privileges, including the leaseholds, joint control of railroads, the right to ship military personnel and equipment across Manchuria from Siberia to its re-established naval base at Port Arthur, etc., it is hard to see just what this provision about "full Chinese sovereignty" could mean.

It is said in justification of these actions by Roosevelt and Churchill that, if Stalin's claims in Manchuria had not been agreed to voluntarily, he would have taken them forcefully from China. But this would of course have been much better than for the Western leaders simply to give away China's territory and possessions, particularly since they did not consult China in the matter beforehand. For Russia to take these objectives by force would merely have been robbery by force, whereas in the view of

every patriotic Chinese, what Stalin, Roosevelt, and
Churchill actually did was robbery by conspiracy and
blackmail.

Where, indeed, was China's supposed Great Power
status now? Did Roosevelt imagine that he could buy off
Stalin into abandoning the Chinese Communists merely
by getting his signature on a treaty with the Chinese
Nationalists? If so, he would have been bitterly disillusioned if he had lived to witness the near future. And it
could logically be asked, if the United States wanted to
buy off aggressors with the Chinese territory of Manchuria, why this had not been done vis-à-vis Japanese aggression there in 1931. The least that would have happened, if real support by us of the Republic of China at
Yalta had forced Stalin into an act of territorial aggression in Manchuria, would have been another Stimson
nonrecognition policy. This would have put our postwar
relations with the Soviet Union on a far more realistic
basis, even if a more uncomfortable one.

Roosevelt wanted to bring Stalin into the emerging
postwar international organization, and doubtless thought
a Far Eastern understanding with her to be necessary to
this.

As can be imagined, the impact of the Yalta agreement
was most severe in China, where the public and private
leadership of the country became completely disillusioned
with the West by its callous buying and selling of China's
flesh and blood, of China's territory. The whole Pacific
war had begun in Japan's aggression in Manchuria. It
was now to end in substituting the Soviets there instead.
The very political basis of the party that governed China,
the Nationalists, lay in its drive to preserve and recover
full rights of self-government everywhere on Chinese
territory. Not even those powers of the West, who had so
long stood for this very thing for China, could now be depended upon to uphold these values in the face of Communist aggression. More and more, the Chinese leadership
at all levels began to be tainted with doubts about Western
nationalism and everything it stood for. Perhaps, they
reasoned, Communism, with its idea of the eventual destruction of the nation-state system, was right, was the
"wave of the future." If to go Communist would make
China a satellite of the Soviet Union, it was probable at

least that this could be a dependable relationship, whereas by now it appeared clear that China's dependency upon the Western powers could not be made to pay off in such coin as China's national sovereignty and territorial integrity.

The U.S. Intervention in Internal Chinese Politics, 1945-1947. Clarence W. Gauss was replaced as Ambassador in Chungking by Patrick J. Hurley in November 1944. Efforts were made to harmonize the badly deteriorated relations between President Chiang and the American military in China. General A. C. Wedemeyer succeeded General Stilwell in command of American forces and did much to improve matters. Efforts to promote war production in China met almost insuperable obstacles. But efforts still went on to unify the Chinese military forces for the defeat of Japan and to make the necessary political accommodations between Nationalists and Communists to allow this.

The notion was fostered by the Russians at this time, that the Chinese Communists were not really Communists, and had no relation to the Soviet Union or international Communism. Many Americans were taken in by this, and many of whose who were not seemed to hope that if the Communists could get into power alongside the Nationalists, they could be "weaned away" from whatever connection they might have with the Soviets and become genuine Chinese Nationalists and believers in parliamentary democracy. But to the Nationalists, all this could mean was that the Chinese Communists would then lose Russian support, and if this was true, why compromise with them? To the Communists, the evidence seemed convincing that American support to the National Government would be jeopardized *unless* that Government were "reformed" by their joining it in a coalition. But if this was true, surely the Communists would never join, trusting that their American friends would blame the Nationalists for this.

Since the United States had been committed to the support of the National Government all along, Ambassador Hurley fell back upon this basic policy more and more as the possibility of a Communist-Nationalist rapprochement waned. At this point he came into conflict with Foreign Service Officers of the State Department in China who wanted to persist in bringing pressure upon the Government to "reform," with threats of support to the Communists. He got some of these officers sent home, where they continued to promote their views in the Department of State. Others remained in the China-Burma-India area. Hurley attributed to their influence a shift which he asserted was taking place away from support to the Government of China and toward support for the Communists. He resigned in frustration, on November 26, 1945.

In early 1946 General George Marshall was sent to China to continue efforts to bring the Communists and Nationalists together in some sort of coalition, so as to end the civil war and begin national reconstruction with United States aid. By dint of great efforts on his part a truce to end current fighting in the civil war was signed on January 10, 1946, but it lasted only a very short time. Both sides were fighting most of the time, but only the Nationalists were subject to United States sanctions in support of the truce. For example, Chiang Kai-shek ordered an offensive against Communists in Inner Mongolia. In October 1946 the United States embargoed the shipment of $75,000,000 worth of munitions to China. That same month all attempts to negotiate were ended and General Marshall returned to the United States early in 1947.

He publicly stated that the failure to bring the CCP and the Government together in a coalition government was due to the resistance and obstruction of extremists on both sides. (*See Reading No. 14.*) Who were these extremists? On the Communist side were these extremists more extreme than Mao Tse-tung himself, who in 1939 had stated the policy of "simultaneous coöperation and struggle with the bourgeoisie," and who had said that the struggle would be "peaceful and bloodless" during periods of coöperation with the Kuomintang but would turn into "armed struggle as soon as [not if] we are compelled to break with the bourgeoisie"? If Mao was that "extreme," just who in the CCP did Marshall think would dare to be less so? And under the terms set by Mao himself in 1939: "We have joined the United Front in order to wage the armed struggle (against the bourgeoisie) more effectively," what member of the Nationalist party could be any less "extreme" than to refuse to join in a coalition with the Communists?

Nationalist Collapse and Communist Takeover in China, 1947-1949.   After March 1947, the Communists brought into action their troops which the Soviets, in violation of their treaty with the Government, had supplied with captured Japanese arms in Manchuria. The Government forces were low on supplies due to American embargo. President Chiang was advised to cut his losses by withdrawing from Manchuria, but refused, and expended much precious material there in a costly stalemate. In central and south China, Red guerrillas blockaded the cities, cutting supplies and disastrously heightening the inflation of currency. This demoralized all classes, and rapidly made the Government's finances bankrupt.

In late 1948 the chief Government commander in North China surrendered for lack of munitions. As early as July, his troops had averaged three to five cartridges per man. North China could have been held if munitions had been supplied him as recommended by all U.S. representatives in China and approved by the Joint Chiefs of Staffs in Washington. Some five months after the action had been approved only ten per cent of these supplies had arrived and they turned out to be largely worthless unusable junk! This failure in American aid broke the back of Government resistance, and by the spring of 1949 the Reds had crossed the Yangtze. By the end of that year their conquest of the mainland was virtually complete. The Government evacuated to Taiwan with some 500,000 armed forces, largely lacking in munitions. The fall of Taiwan to the Communists was widely prophesied in Washington, and the State Department circulated to U.S. embassies abroad a statement in which the takeover of Taiwan by the Communists was predicted. To "let the dust settle" seemed to be all our government was prepared to do.

— 4 —

COMMUNISM VERSUS FREEDOM IN CHINA, 1949-1959

The Communist Government in China. In September 1949, before total takeover in mainland China, the Communist regime was established in Peking, under the title of The Peoples' Republic of China (PRC). Mao Tse-tung was President of the Government Council and actual head of the regime. Chou En-lai was Premier, and Chu Teh was Vice-Chairman of the Military Council (under Mao) and Commanding Officer of the Armed Forces. Control of the regime was concentrated in the hands of these persons and of a small core of their trusted associates including such persons as Liu Shao-ch'i, Li Li-san, Liu Po-cheng, Lin Piao, and P'eng Teh-huai. All these personages were then and have remained, Soviet-oriented Stalinists, dedicated to the Communist world revolution. (*See Reading No. 15.*)

The Chinese Communist Party (CCP) under them at the time numbered somewhat less than 3,000,000 members. Between 1949 and 1959 it expanded to nearly 8,000,000, organized into local and regional subdivisions and culminating in the Central Executive Committee. The CCP is actually governed by the Central Political Bureau of which Mao Tse-tung was first Chairman, under the principle of "Democratic Centralism." Under this principle, which rules also in the government, policy questions may be discussed at all levels but decisions are made only at the top, after which the decisions are not subject to further question. (*See Reading No. 16.*).

Through the interlocking directorates of CCP and PRC, the party oligarchy actually controls the government and through it governs the "people." The "people" includes all Communists and non-Communists, who supposedly enjoy civil and political rights, but anti-Communists are specifically excluded from such privileges and are, in fact, beyond the pale of organized society and government. They are outlaws. Since anyone who opposes what the party and government want is classed as anti-Communist, it is clear that such civil and political rights as the "people" enjoy are limited to those who submissively obey the established dictatorship, and who thus by definition can possess no independent civil rights at all. In the PRC, the ultimate guarantee against the development of independent civil rights in the hands of the masses lies in the complete integration of judicial and political processes with the former subordinated to the latter at all times.

In spite of their seeming contempt for the rule of law, the Chinese Communists still retain a place in their system of government for charters and constitutions. In September 1949, they adopted the so-called "Common Program," a statement of basic aims for the future, suitably vague as to specific structures of government, and embodying the United Front tactic so as to secure coöperation in immediate tasks from all those non-Communists surviving from the previous regime. In September 1956, they adopted a "Constitution," which reflected their plans for increasing growth of a Communist society in China. It is a testimony to the need of all political regimes for stability that even the most totalitarian of them expresses its most temporary tactical policies in terms of "fundamental laws" or "constitutions." Like that of the U.S.S.R., the Chinese Communist Constitution can be disregarded, violated, or broken at any time at the discretion of the supreme dictator of the party or government.

Economic Development in Communist China, 1949-1959. The basic economic aim of the CCP is to develop state power so as to strengthen its control in China and help the Communist Bloc to extend the Communist world revolution. For these purposes the economics of welfare have been subordinated to the economics of warfare. Forced industrialization has been the consistent policy throughout. At the start, the government concerned itself principally with rehabilitation of the war-ruined economic facilities, particularly in agriculture and communications. As industry gradually went back into operation, the government extended its controls over it. The Provisional Regulations for Private Enterprises promulgated in December 1950 embodied a system of Government controls, not of government operation. But by 1953 state ownership had been extended to the sources of more than one half of all industrial production. Since then a small sector of private enterprise in industry has been preserved, largely for political reasons, to give the appearance of diversity and to serve as a possible lure to attract able Chinese businessmen to return from abroad. At the same time, tight controls have been imposed on consumption, through taxation, price-fixing, and manipulation of distribution, in order to maximize savings for investment in new enterprises according to government plan. In the case of food, shelter, and clothing, the controls on consumption provide a powerful lever against possible dissidence among an increasingly deprived people.

Between 1952 and 1955 state planning was formalized into the first Five Year Plan, adopted on July 30, 1955, to cover the period 1953-1957. Under this plan heavy industry was primary and consumer industries strictly secondary. Military power was to be developed; and Soviet methods were adopted, including the forced collectivisation of the peasants, heavy taxation, and strict control of all trade. At the termination of this plan the second Five Year Plan took over, to cover the period 1958-1962, with similar aims. State ownership and operation of the means of production has proceeded steadily under these plans.

There is no doubt that production has greatly increased in Communist China in the last ten years. At the same time, consumption has sunk to what are probably all-time lows. For example, even with a rapidly increasing population and very little increase in the area of land under cultivation, Communist China has been able to export large quantities of foodstuffs to pay for necessary capital imports and to wage economic war over some neutralist areas of southern Asia. The costs in mass deprivation have been huge, even for a people accustomed to very low standards of living. Much of the economic gain has been secured through "crisis" measures, available only once. Such, for example, were the large amounts of money confiscated during organized drives against private business during the Korean war. Such, perhaps, is also the present communalization of the peasants which, according to the Communists, has resulted in more than 100,-000,000 peasant families being taken from their homes, placed in dormitories, deprived of almost every bit of personal property, and made to work on the now state-owned collective farms.

Such drastic expedients as this would seem to approach close to the edge of potential feasibility. Such gains as are thus registered are probably "once only" possibilities. How much they are economic, and how much political and social measures, is only speculative at present. The burden they place upon administration must be immense, and probably will increase as these total measures arouse more and more resistance and less and less coöperation from the peasantry. And the more organizational resources are committed to the management of huge enterprises like this, the greater the tendency will be to decrease thus the net production and other economic gains therefrom.

Just what is the meaning of Communist China's economic gains in the last ten years? The main emphasis continues to be upon military power and heavy industry, with general disregard of the desires of the masses for a better living. Arms and industry are being constructed out of the flesh and blood of the peasantry, and for what purpose? In crude terms of the prevention of major uprisings of the masses, the amount of military power in the hands of the government is already more than enough. Its aims doubtless go much further than this, to include the takeover by threat of force or actual force, of numerous surrounding areas such as South Korea, South Vietnam, Taiwan, Malaya, and Thailand. These would be merely the earlier steps in the general extension of Communist revolution, to which the increasing power of Communist China seems clearly dedicated, in concert with that of the Communist Bloc.

Organizations and Chinese Communist Party Control. Mass organizations are a major feature of the CCP control mechanism in China. Most of these organizations are especially created for the purpose of supporting the CCP, but all of them in effect do this, whatever their ostensible primary purpose. To have some of these organizations less directly related to the CCP serves a useful

purpose by fostering the psychological illusions of a
"united front," and thus making some of the organizations
more useful abroad for infiltration and subversion.

All these mass organizations have one basic purpose,
namely to help in subordinating the interests of individuals and groups to that of the state. There are mass
organizations of every possible type, including, for
example, the New Democratic Youth League for ages
fourteen to twenty-five, with 14,000,000 members; the
All China Federation of Democratic Women, with 80,-
000,000 members; the Sino-Soviet Friendship Association
which, in 1954, had 68,000,000 members organized in
200,000 branches. Their purposes include such things
as the mobilization of workers and the improvement of
their products, the control of students, the promotion of
hostility to the United States, the elimination of incompe-
tent bureaucrats, the regimentation of religions and their
followers, and the final elimination of religious beliefs.
In every case, whatever the ostensible leadership, control
over them is in the hands of dependable party personnel.

**Ideological Regimentation in Communst China,
1949-1959.** Regimentation of thought in Communist
China has depended steadily upon terror as its ultimate
sanction. Terror, in fact, has an ideological meaning in
itself, related to the warlike character of Communism
which holds that the ultimate aim of politics is the extermination of the opposition. To give this threat real
substance is the vast and complex police system, reaching down into every village and into every city street.
It is directly and completely controlled by the party,
which tries to see to it that everyone who in any way
resists persuasion and propaganda is treated as a counter-
revolutionary or "reactionary." The minimum penalty is
to be sent into a forced labor camp similar to those established in the U.S.S.R. For those deemed hopelessly un-
regenerate, quick liquidation is the rule, with or without
any legal proceedings. Organized campaigns against such
individuals have been instituted, such as the "Counter-
revolutionary Suppression Campaign" of 1950 and 1951;
the so-called "Three Anti Movement (anti-corruption,
waste, and bureaucratism) in 1951; the so-called "Five
Anti Movement" (anti-bribery, tax evasion, fraud, theft of
government property, and theft of state economic secrets)

lasting from October 1951 to June 1952. Millions of persons have lost their lives in these campaigns of terror.

Thus, the success or failure of propaganda efforts by the government depend not upon any intrinsic appeals of the propaganda, and not upon the technical competence of the indoctrination methods, but fundamentally upon the punishments that are seen to fall upon those who resist. Every possible medium of persuasion and indoctrination that can be mobilized seems to have been utilized. Radio is useful in view of widespread illiteracy, but is hampered by dialect differences around the country. The press, editorial policy of which is set in Peking, reaches directly only the educated minority. Book and periodical publication are extensive, with very wide government participation, and much direct and indirect assistance from the U.S.S.R.

Theater and films are perhaps costly, but have the benefit of almost universal applicability. Art forms of all kind must carry the Communist party message. Emphasis upon form must always give way to the carriage of political content. There is no "art for art's sake" in Communist China, any more than there is learning for learning's sake. (*See Reading No. 17.*)

Education, actually, is very difficult to distinguish from the more overt and direct efforts at ideological regimentation. Perhaps the main difference is that education does attempt to transmit technical knowledge in addition to being a form of indoctrination. Even purely educational problems, such as the elimination of illiteracy, the reform of language and writing, the construction of educational facilities, and the supply of educators, are difficult enough in themselves. But all of them are made more complicated by the vast and all pervasive political overlay under which they exist. No independent education free from government control is tolerated. All students and teachers come directly under the control of the party. In September 1951, an intensive campaign was put on against all teachers, to make them completely submissive to Communist ideology and to party control, prior to using them to train large numbers of party workers for government position, jobs in mass organizations, etc. The method was that of "brainwashing" which basically means group criticism of the individual carried on until he is brought to criticize

himself and confesses his errors. This is used both as
remedial measure and to keep in line those whose orthodoxy has already been established.

In early 1957, Mao Tse-tung, seemingly against the
advice of some close associates, tried an experiment in
freeing speech and expression, the so-called "Let 100
Flowers Bloom" campaign. He seemed to trust and believe
that he had sufficient genuine support among intellectuals
so that their statements and writings, even if critical,
would still be friendly. He was to be greatly disappointed,
as many came out with statements so hostile to the
regime and to the party that Mao was soon forced to
terminate his experiment with limited freedom of speech.
Great numbers of students and teachers were removed
from their schools and sent to the country as agricultural
laborers. There were numerous liquidations and a number
of student revolts were put down by violence. Limited
"liberalization" of speech and opinion thus had a short
unhappy life in Communist China, and it is doubtful that
such an experiment will soon be tried again. Grievances
must be submerged, perhaps to come out again only under
the most severe pressures.

**Agrarian Revolution in Communist China, 1949-
1959.**   The Agrarian Reform Act of June 1950, designed
to bring about the redistribution of land, was at first
applied in such a way as to leave even landlords enough
land to support a family, and it left medium-sized holdings alone. But by October 1950, it was being applied in
such a way as to deprive completely all large and medium
holders of their land and other property which was divided
up and distributed. Even small farmers had their land confiscated. The entire campaign developed into a series of
mob demonstrations and denunciations followed by hasty
arraignments and staged trials, after which landowners
were slaughtered and their property distributed. This resulted in a large increase in the number of small farmers
living on the edge of subsistence.

Since the government could quickly tax them to the
edge of starvation and could requisition as much of their
produce as it wished after taxes, these farmers soon began
to turn back their newly acquired property deeds to the
authorities. They were under the double squeeze of the
government, which in addition to taxes and requisitions,

could and did impose high prices on commodities the farmers had to buy. Revolts broke out, but were quickly suppressed. Per capita production doubtless declined.

By 1955 the regime was ready for the next step toward communization. They instituted "coöperation," that is, coöperative production with individual farmers paid for their labor. There was to be no private ownership or sale of the crops coöperatively produced on individual plots of land. Finally, in 1957-1958 the regime instituted the "communalization" program. Under it all farms were merged into communes, and farmhouses were torn down. The peasants were transferred into dormitories where they literally owned nothing but the clothes on their backs. They were fed in commune dining halls and their children were cared for in commune nurseries. By late 1958 the regime announced that more than 100,000,000 farm families had thus been "communalized."

What did the Chinese Communists aim at here? No doubt some economies could be secured. Razing millions of farm houses and housing the peasantry in barracks could free some land for cultivation. Collective feeding of millions of persons could secure some economies in the procurement, transportation, and processing of staple foodstuffs. Control of production and the collection of the crops by the government would be simplified. All these things would greatly increase the number of civil and military functionaries in the countryside to carry out these measures.

In addition, the commune system of living subjected the individual peasants to complete and all-pervasive control twenty-four hours a day. Perhaps the most important result of the communalization of 100,000,000 peasant families is the complete obliteration of their privacy and individuality, in favor of communist "integration" and the unlimited and complete service of the state and party. When, in addition, we find that the communes have a military character, each one being organized as a militia unit, the overwhelmingly feudalistic character of all this emerges clearly. The recent history of the Chinese farming masses can be justly titled "From Peasantry to Peonage." This is veritable slavery.

What can or will the peasantry do about all this? Overt violent resistance is impossible. On the other hand, passive resistance and unenthusiastic "coöperation" are highly probable, and in them the economies of the system can soon be swallowed up. Net losses are likely to ensue, raising the question of what new and even more drastic expedient the Communists can next initiate, and, in turn, the question of how farmers will react to that.

Some Cultural Developments in Communist China. As early as 1949 the Chinese Communists, with characteristic attention to organization, were holding a Cultural Conference, from which emerged the All-China Federation of Literary and Art Circles. A second national cultural conference was held during September and October 1953. Thus the regime moved to include cultural matters in its total system of control. At first there were some struggles among the Chinese Communists for the control of literature and the arts. Examples were made of the losers in order to bring into line the great number of writers and artists not in the party or administration. The results can be seen in the case of historical writing and research under the Chinese Communists. Under the guise of "re-interpretation," history was to be brought into line with Stalinist Communism.

In religion, where the Communists had the established institutions to work on, the first step was to cut off all religious groups from support and contacts abroad. Most foreign Christian missionaries left China, but many were detained and tried on various charges ranging from espionage to murder of Chinese infants in orphanages. Some died in captivity and others were expelled. The next step was to set up so-called "Reform Churches" to be used by the Communists for the nonreligious purposes of pushing Communist ideology and advancing the Communist program in economics and politics. All religions were included in this. Buddhism and Mohammedanism have much larger followings in China than Christianity, and proportionately greater attention has been given to bringing them under complete Communist control and making them into instruments of the regime. The Chinese Islamic Religious Association, one of the "Reform" religious groups, was organized by the regime to promote Communism.

Basic Communist opposition to religion lies in the fact that religion by its very nature is an individual and personal matter, and that Communism stands for the destruction of the individual personality in favor of the state and the Communist party. Communism cannot tolerate a personal relationship between man and God, and it must destroy all religion. Measures to this end in Communist China have been far more ruthlessly pervasive than anything done in the U.S.S.R. The impact of these measures is, however, still difficult to determine. Religion may yet survive in the minds and hearts of millions of Chinese, but its institutional life has been completely subverted to the purposes of an atheist materialist state. (*See Reading No. 18.*)

International cultural relations are an important feature of Communist China. Under formal intergovernmental agreements with the Soviet Union and the Eastern European satellites, regular programs of cultural exchange are carried on in education, theater, student exchanges, and exhibitions. Neutralist states of south Asia are also included in these activities whenever possible.

Foreign Relations of Communist China, 1949-1959. Mao Tse-tung declared the basic alignment of Communist China with the Soviet Union in June 1949, and on February 14, 1950, the treaty of alliance between the two countries was signed. (*See Reading No. 19.*) Since then the Moscow-Peking Axis has weathered all storms and today is doubtless stronger than ever. It is the power of the U.S.S.R. standing behind Communist China which makes Mao Tse-tung's regime such a threat to world peace and freedom. By itself, Communist China is a third-rate power militarily and a vast poorhouse as to economics. It cannot soon achieve great power status.

The Moscow-Peking alliance, like other alliances, has lasted because the two members of it need each other. The Chinese Communist regime owes its very existence to the U.S.S.R. In the words of Mao Tse-tung: "Do you seriously think that it was possible for us to come out victorious without the Soviet Union? Decidedly not." And as his regime has continued, Mao has intensified his military and economic dependence upon the Soviets. At the same time he has conclusively rejected so-called national Communism, or Titoism.

The Chinese Communists have convincingly turned their backs on nationalism of any type, in favor of ortho-

dox Communist world universalism. In this vein they
strongly back the repression of all nationalistic tendencies
in the European satellites of the U.S.S.R., while setting
up the beginnings of their own subsatellite system in
North Korea and North Vietnam. Thus they make
themselves increasingly valuable to the U.S.S.R., the center of the Communist movement for world revolution.
And their value is increased by their contribution to the
work of winning over neutralists in other Asian countries,
who would be less susceptible to a direct approach by the
U.S.S.R.

Toward the non-Communist countries of the West the
attitude of the Chinese Communists is "correct" and
wholly rational within their own framework of ideas and
interest. Since their dominant drive is always toward the
destruction of the non-Communist world and the substitution in all cases of Communist regimes, they are
always destructive and aggressive toward the free world.
Since the United States is the main center of free-world
strength, toward it their hostility must be the most
open and severe. They attempt by war and the threat of
atomic war to blackmail the United States into abandoning
all military defense against Communist aggression. They
hope in this way to achieve piecemeal surrender to them
of all areas and positions now held by non-Communist
Asian regimes, such as those in Japan, South Korea, Taiwan, the Philippines, South Vietnam, Thailand, and Malaya.

Since in all these areas the United States has undertaken defensive commitments, the objective of the Chinese
Communists must be to weaken the will and resolution of
the American people and their government to make good
on them. A Communist takeover in all these areas, and
their economic and military amalgamation with Communist China, is the primary objective of Sino-Russian
policy. This would build up Communist China, particularly in the economic field, to where, particularly in combination with the U.S.S.R., it would have a preponderance
of power in respect to the free world.

**United States Policy Toward Communist China,
1949-1959.** As the Nationalists were driven off the mainland and the Communists established their control there,
the United States government had to face squarely the

problem of relations with the new Chinese regime. During the second half of 1949 this matter was under intensive study in the Department of State. When the British recognized Communist China in early 1950, quick United States recognition was predicted. Why did this not happen? Admittedly, the Communists scandalously mistreated our diplomats, and they confiscated our diplomatic properties in China. But these actions and other measures against our businessmen and missionaries in China were no worse than those leveled against British subjects, for example. But the public reaction in the United States against these affronts was much stronger than in Britain. Recognition might have come within a year or so, at that, but in the meantime the Chinese Communists entered the Korean war and were branded as aggressors by the United Nations. They have never purged themselves of this transgression against international law and morality.

The official U.S. policy of nonrecognition of Communist China has been firmly based upon two facts which are not likely to change soon. First, the Chinese Communists do not control all of China, and there is on the Chinese soil of Taiwan an alternative Chinese government which is preferable to the Communist regime on all counts and which represents the hope of China for freedom. Second, the Chinese Communists have consistently proven in action their stated policy of violating all accepted canons of international behavior, and they declare their constant aim to be the destruction of the United States. (*See Reading No. 22.*)

After the Korean war began, and particularly after the entry of the Chinese Communists into it, the policy of the United States took a more positive turn, toward support of the Republic of China on Taiwan. Under the terms of our military alliance of 1955 with the Republic of China, and the authorization given the President by joint resolution of Congress in 1955, we have now given a general indication that any attempt by the Chinese Communists to seize the offshore island groups of Matsu and Quemoy will be met by U.S. armed resistance. In the summer and fall of 1958, the United States was on the verge of another war with Communist China over this issue. The British government, though feeling that these islands should be given over to the Chinese Communists, supported our stand against any solution to the problem being imposed by the Chinese Communists by force. The position was also openly supported by our main allies in the Far East, including Japan, the Republic of Korea, and the Philippines. As the Communists have always maintained, their pressure on the offshore islands is only part of a campaign to secure Taiwan and liquidate the free government there. To this the United States government and people are frontally opposed, with preponderance of world opinion on their side. As long as the government and people on Taiwan prosper with our help, there will always be danger of war with the Chinese Communists.

The Republic of China Takes over Taiwan, 1945-1950. The Cairo Declaration of December 1, 1943, stated the purpose of "The Three Great Allies," China, the United Kingdom, and the United States "that all the territories Japan has stolen from the Chinese, such as Manchuria, Formosa [Taiwan], and the Pescadores, shall be restored to the Republic of China." Under international law, this was clearly not a mere statement of intent, but a binding commitment. As part of the terms of the Japanese surrender, the Potsdam Proclamation of July 26, 1945, stated (paragraph 8) "The terms of the Cairo Declaration shall be carried out," and when Japan agreed to these terms of surrender she agreed to turn back to China all those territories she had taken previously. Under arrangements made by the Supreme Commander for the Allied Powers, the Republic of China did take over in Taiwan from the Japanese, and in this way the island was returned to China after some fifty years in Japanese hands.

Although China was not a signatory of the general peace treaty with Japan, she made a separate peace, and in this treaty between the Republic of China and Japan dated April 28, 1952, it was recognized that "all treaties, conventions and agreements concluded before December 9, 1941, between Japan and China have become null and void as a consequence of the war." This would include the treaty after the Sino-Japanese War, in 1895, under which Taiwan was ceded to Japan, and would mean that since, as a result of the war, the cession was null and void, Taiwan had reverted to Chinese ownership. To question this would be to question the postwar disposition of all other territories of China formerly held by Japan, including Manchuria which is now in the hands of the Chinese Communists who took it from the government of Chiang Kai-shek.

Early administration of Taiwan by the Chinese government was extremely bad. The first administrator of the island, later shot as a Communist collaborator, set up a "carpet-bagging" regime characterized by looting, government monopolies in business, and neglect and abuse of the people. Eventually, violence broke out, and many of the local leaders who had welcomed the return of their island to China were massacred. More than 10,000 people lost their lives in savage retaliation.

In 1948 General Chen Cheng was sent to Taiwan to prepare it for the retreat there of the National Government. When the mainland fell some 1.5-2,000,000 armed forces and civilians fled there with the Government, which began to operate there in December 1949. The Communists took some of the offshore islands such as Chusan and Hainan, but were heavily repelled in October 1949 when trying to overrun Quemoy. They made large preparations seemingly directed at taking Taiwan. The State Department evacuated the dependents of its personnel there and seemed to anticipate Communist takeover. The armed forces of the Republic of China on Taiwan were in a bad state of disorganization and lacked weapons and supplies.

In January 1950, Secretary of State Acheson announced that Taiwan and South Korea were both outside the American line of defense in the western Pacific, but that in event of attack they could appeal to the United Nations. American forces were withdrawn from Korea in 1949, and President Truman, in January 1950, refused to provide military supplies for Taiwan or to involve our forces in its defense. Such was the position in June 1950 when the Korean war began.

Political Development in Free China, 1949-1959. After the Government moved there in 1949, Taiwan was the center of the National Government of the Republic of China, and at the same time was governed as a province of China. The National government is largely controlled by personnel from the mainland, including some 1,200 of the 3,000 representatives in the National Assembly. The whole apparatus of the Government exists in Taiwan, where much of its energy is devoted to planning for the eventual return to power in mainland China. Since this Government is one which claims sovereignty over the mainland, its personnel is and must be of and from the provinces on the mainland. Its location in Taiwan, in the mind of the Government, cannot make it merely a Taiwan government, any more than the location of the seat of federal government of the United States in Washington, D.C., makes that the government merely of the District of Columbia.

Contrasted with the National Government, the provincial government of Taiwan is increasingly in the hands of the Taiwan people. This development has been slow, and complete autonomy in the provincial government still does not exist. But by 1958, of twenty-one mayors of large cities and prefectural magistrates, nineteen were Taiwan-born. Of 1,025 prefectural and municipal assembly members, 923, or more than ninety per cent, are Taiwan-born. Elections for these assemblies are held every three years. In January 1958, 78.31 per cent of all qualified voters cast ballots. Secret ballot and majority rule have become general in the conduct of government affairs in Taiwan. The Nationalist party (Kuomintang) has now built up a strong organization among the Taiwan people, and its candidates from among their number are likely to win. The conduct of government in Taiwan demonstrates both efficiency and progress to the goal of democracy and self-government.

Strong open criticism of government is frequent in Taiwan. Some of it is pointed and realistic, but a great deal is vague, cloudy, and general. Specific issues and problems are likely to be tackled in a direct way, but much of the discussion shows little real understanding of such values as freedom and democracy which are often advocated but little thought out as to local applicability to local problems and in the light of local culture. There is a great deal of unthinking acceptance of everything American, and much equally unthinking rejection of what is traditionally Chinese. This is almost certain to lead to insufficient utilization of the real political and psychological assets inherited from China's past. There is no doubt that American influence is to blame for much of this.

To deal with the constant problem of Communist infiltration there is a strong police organization. Numerous Communist agents have been uncovered and operations against them are continuous. Since the early days of Government takeover, civil order has been constant, based on increasing levels of economic prosperity for the masses and constantly expanding political participation. This should be contrasted with the period of Japanese occupation when, during some fifty years there were some one hundred revolts of varying size.

By now it is a firm conclusion that the Taiwan people are happy with their government and would not welcome any drastic change in it. Localism and provincial separation are never absent entirely from the Chinese political scene, and to this rule Taiwan is no exception. But, in spite of a few dissatisfied émigrés to the contrary, the Taiwan people would today reject the idea of independence from the Republic of China as a solution to their political problems.

Many Americans seem troubled by a problem which really does not exist at all, or certainly not in the way in which they think of it, namely, that of the succession to the Presidency of the Republic of China after Chiang Kai-shek. The answer is that if the President dies in office the Vice-President will succeed as provided in the Constitution of 1947. (*See Reading No. 20.*) Also under the terms of the Constitution, the President cannot succeed himself again. At present the strongest candidate for the office in the next election is the Vice-President who, in the summer of 1958, was appointed Premier. He is well known, among other things, as chiefly responsible for the highly successful agrarian reform in Taiwan.

Some Military Developments in Taiwan, 1949-1959. Between the fall of the mainland in 1949 and May 1951, there was no official United States military advisory group in Taiwan. This policy was confirmed by President Truman in January 1950, when he said we would neither supply Chinese forces in Taiwan nor help defend the island with our own forces. But after the onset of the Korean war the 7th Fleet was ordered by the President to "neutralize" Taiwan, meaning that no Communist attack was to be allowed upon it, and no Nationalist attack could be made upon the Chinese mainland from Taiwan. In July 1950, the Joint Chiefs of Staff held that Taiwan was of strategic importance in United States defense, and recommended military aid there. By 1953 the forces on Taiwan had been strengthened sufficiently so that they were considered able to defend the island.

This was not merely a result of increased supplies from the United States. There was also a great deal of improvement in the general conditions of life for the forces, including food, housing, and medical care. Universal military conscription began to renew the strength of the forces, physically less qualified men being retired. New officer groups were being developed from the high school and college graduates who were taken in by the draft. Constant training was carried on with the advice of American military advisers. A trained reserve was being built up, so that in time of emergency the armed forces could be greatly expanded. But still, as a matter of basic American policy, the posture of the armed forces of the Republic of China was strictly defensive.

In undertaking its responsibilities under the Mutual Defense Treaty of December 1954 (*see Reading No. 21*), the United States reserved to itself the possession and use of such offensive weapons as nuclear devices, heavy bombers, landing craft, attack transports, and naval power with real offensive capability. Considerable defensive air power was built up in the hands of the Chinese, and in the air battles with the Communists in the fall of 1958 Nationalist pilots shot down fourteen Communist fighter pilots for every one of their own pilots lost. This seemed attributable to better flyers using equipment superior to that furnished the Chinese Communists by the Russians.

The United States monopoly of offensive weapons lent a particular importance to the Joint Resolution of Congress, January 1955, under which the President was authorized to use United States forces to defend "related positions and territories" outside Taiwan and the Pescadores, if necessary to the defense of Taiwan and the Pescadores. This decreased the possibility that defense of the Republic of China would be so localized and concentrated on the immediate environs of Taiwan as to make of little use the strategic weapons increasingly available to the United States.

Economic Development of the Republic of China, 1949-1959. By October 31, 1958, the civilian population of Taiwan was 9,965,726. Adding military personnel, the total is well over 10,000,000, a population larger than that of Australia. The annual rate of population increase is 3.6 per cent per year, which will mean doubling the population in about thirty years. This rapid increase in population is based heavily upon two things: greatly improved health conditions and material increases in personal income. This latter is the result of agricultural and industrial development.

Agricultural reform was accomplished between 1949 and 1955, in three stages. Rents were reduced from 55-60 per cent down to 37.5 per cent of annual main crop yield. Government-owned lands were sold to tenant farmers on easy terms. All landlord holdings above seven acres in size were bought by the government and sold to tenants on the installment plan. The landlords were paid in commodities and in bonds issued against industrial properties which the government had taken over from the Japanese. Later these properties were turned over to the shareholders, thus creating a new class of industrial property-owners. At the same time as these reforms radically increased the farmers' share of agricultural income, this income was being raised through large-scale improvement of production.

The Joint Commission on Rural Reconstruction, a Sino-American organization supported by United States foreign aid funds, was responsible for the main features of agricultural reform in Taiwan. Much of its work is done through the Farmers' Associations which exist in every village and serve as combined educational and promotional organizations, financial and consumer coöperatives, depots for crop collection and fertilizer distribution, and centers of organizational work for farmers and their families. All actual farmers are members of the village Association, and above the village and on the level of township, county, and prefecture, the Associations are representative of the lower levels.

Current successes of all this are seen in the figures.

Taiwan annually exports some 200,000 tons of rice and $100,000,000 worth of sugar. Its chief imports are chemical fertilizers, machinery and tools, and crude oil. In the first half of 1958 exports exceeded imports by approximately $20,000,000.

Industrialization in Taiwan has been built on an inherited Japanese plant, mostly in ruins at war's end, plus a skilled labor force also inherited from the period of Japanese control. Both plant and manpower have been greatly expanded since 1949, with United States aid particularly in power, ship-building, communication and transport, chemicals and fertilizers, building materials, petroleum refining, and textiles. The rapidity of industrialization can be seen in the sharply rising use of electric power, the demand for which is rising by eighteen per cent per year. Between 1946 and 1957 electric power output increased five times. Great expansion, chiefly hydroelectric facilities used also for irrigation, is being undertaken.

Can Taiwan become economically self-supporting? The answer is "No," at least not while military expenditures are so high and while the standard of living is being raised steadily at the same time. It is hard to foresee in the near future any substantial change here. The high level of military expenditures and standing forces cannot be dispensed with as long as the Chinese Communists continue their aggressive expansionism in the Far East and continue to devote so much of their own income to the construction of military power. And the steady rise in the standard of living among Taiwan people is a powerful weapon of political warfare against the Communists. It demonstrates how much more effectively the welfare of an Asian people can be promoted by free governments and by peaceful methods than by Communist governmental oppression, terror, and bloodshed. Considering both its military outcomes to date and its political outcomes, the approximately one billion dollars the United States has invested in Taiwan during the past ten years would seem well worth while.

The chief deficiencies of the United States economic aid in Taiwan seem to lie in a certain lack of sensitivity on our part to the sociological and political by-products which our help produces. There is a general lack of attention to the overriding population problem. There is an almost complete lack of understanding on the American side of the evolution of social organizations and social control under the impact of ideological and technical change. Whether we can develop a sophisticated approach to these matters may well determine the eventual success or failure of our economic assistance there.

Social and Cultural Developments in the Republic of China, 1949-1959. Japanese cultural policy in Taiwan was one of "Japanization." Primary education was Japanese, and a peak of about 71 per cent attendance of all primary school-age children was attained. Thus the Japanese language became a generally used second language everywhere. On the higher levels educational opportunities were monopolized by the Japanese, and very few Taiwan Chinese went to high school and still fewer to college. By contrast, in 1957-1958, nearly 95 per cent of all primary school-age children attended the compulsory and state-supported schools. There were 1,537 primary schools, with 35,298 teachers and 1,480,000 students. There were some 250,000 students in public and private high schools, entry to which was through competitive examinations. Some twenty private and state colleges and universities enrolled nearly 27,000 students on undergraduate, graduate, and professional levels in 1958-1959.

These figures are impressive, but qualitative improvement has a long way to go. The system of education has expanded very quickly at all levels. Many teachers came over from the mainland, and many more are being trained. But they are paid very poorly as, indeed, are all civil servants. This is caused by the burden on the government of military expenditures. Most teachers work outside their schools in order to make both ends meet. At the college and university level this means that professors have little or no time for study and research. There is a general lack of laboratories, libraries, and research facilities. The inevitable result is a general decline in the intellectual vitality of those who have the responsibility for creating the moral and intellectual attitudes of the future generation. The situation here is going from bad to worse. Much of the best talent is lost since many of the very best university graduates go abroad to study and remain there, attracted by better pay and working conditions. It has been suggested that the United States government, in coöperation with the authorities in Taiwan, should work out arrangements whereby students coming here for study will return to Taiwan. Current rules and regulations are loosely drawn and laxly enforced. By contrast to these problems on the higher levels, the general literacy rate in Taiwan is 90 per cent, and illiteracy is expected to be entirely wiped out in ten years. The Chinese national language, based on Peking dialect of Mandarin, is taught in all schools.

In spite of technical and financial obstacles, basic research does go on, and there is considerable publication of all kinds. Approximately 1,500 new titles appear each year. Much of this is of excellent quality, especially that in the historical and literary fields. There are over 600 magazines and 500,000 copies of daily newspapers printed in Taiwan. Government supervision of their contents to guard against subversive actions does not prevent these publications from printing strong criticisms of government policy.

Radio and moving picture production are active in Taiwan. Of some forty broadcasting stations, about one quarter are government operated. About 200 moving pictures are produced yearly in Taiwan, both short subjects and full-length features. Numerous films are imported from Japan and the United States. There is no television.

Traditional arts, such as calligraphy and painting, are actively pursued. Great collections of Chinese classical antiquities, painting, porcelains, bronzes, calligraphy, and old and rare books, were brought over from the mainland and are being opened to a very interested local public which has never before had the chance to see these relics of China's historic culture. In both music and painting the traditional forms are being preserved, while Western influences are appearing in current production.

Traditional Chinese religions seem far more strongly established in Taiwan than had been the case in recent years on the mainland. There are more than 3,000 temples of the Buddhist and Taoist religions and of various local divinities, with millions of believers. There are 200,000 Roman Catholic converts and 100,000

Protestant communicants. About 40,000 Moslems live in Taiwan. All people enjoy freedom of religion. Perhaps the most rapidly growing religion in Taiwan today is Roman Catholicism, which carries on its work everywhere.

Civic and cultural organizations of all sorts also flourish in Taiwan. Trade unions include 250,000 members in more than 600 unions, and in general relations between labor and management are good. A national social security system is gradually developing, about one fifth of the population now being covered by its provisions. All government employees and their families are already covered. Farmers are all members of the Farmers' Associations in every village, and their representatives govern the Associations at the township, county, and prefectural levels. These Associations sponsor 3,000 4-H Clubs with 36,000 members from the farm youths. These Farm Associations are locally self-governing. In all these organizations and in private life, women enjoy equality in law and status. Five hundred women hold high office in national and local government, including two women judges of the Supreme Court. There are 20,000 women teachers, including 972 on college and university faculties. Many are in the professions.

The Problem of China Today. As of early 1959, only a small minority of the American people support any solution of the China problem in terms of complete Communist victory, involving Communist takeover of Taiwan, plus admission to the United Nations and United States recognition followed by a program of economic aid to the Communists. Parts of such a Communist victory are supported by somewhat larger numbers of people in this country, particularly those aspects involving United States recognition and United Nations admission. Recognition is usually supported by its limited number of proponents as a "realistic" policy in view of *de facto* control over the Chinese mainland by the Communist regime. And U.N. admission is usually justified by its supporters on grounds that the U.N. should be fully representative of all governments and regimes and that none should be excluded therefrom. (*See Reading No. 22.*)

A still different minority of the American people, on

the other hand, are advocates of immediate war with the Chinese Communists and are willing to risk a third world war in order to attempt the destruction of Chinese Communism now, before it becomes any more powerful than it is today. They justify this view by pointing out that the longer overt hostilities are delayed, the stronger the enemy is bound to become. The time to strike, they say, is now.

Contrasted with these two minority views on the China problem today are the views of the vast majority of the American people. To them, and particularly to those who have even a moderate factual knowledge of China, the Communist regime there represents a reversion to despotism, but to a despotism unprecedented in Chinese history. On the other hand, although they recognize shortcomings and faults in the Republic of China on Taiwan, they recognize that it embodies genuine progress toward political freedom and devotion to human welfare.

Judged from the viewpoint of liberal democracy there can be little doubt that the government and society on Taiwan today is so vastly preferable to the Communist regime on the mainland that the free world should enthusiastically support it against its much larger and more powerful opponent.

Today, however, the free world limits itself at the most to repelling the aggressive initiatives of the Communists against the Republic of China, and recoils at the prospect of further wars. In respect to China, as in Korea and Germany, the United States and its chief allies seem resigned at the most to a policy of military protection of the territorial status quo, combined with economic and political support of South Korea, West Germany, and Taiwan. The more positive concept of carrying even economic and political warfare to the enemy comes under increasing attack from the allies of the United States and from those elements in the United States who believe that the mitigation of hostility between the Communist world and the free world is feasible and desirable. These governments and people evidently do not accept the Communist analysis according to which "Bolsheviks and their enemies—all non-Bolsheviks—have essentially nothing in common; there is no shared standard of value between and above them." (N. Leites, *A Study of Bolshevism*, Glencoe, Ill., 1953, p. 61).

It always seems tempting to many men of good-will in the West to try to disprove this Communist analysis and to alleviate east-west tensions by advancing as far as possible toward the satisfaction of the interests and demands of the Communists. Yet it is doubtful whether any such policy would work better with the Communists than with Hitler. In either case, the result is likely to be the same, namely, that we would run out of material with which to appease demands based upon a plan for total takeover, and that the other side would help force the development of such a position through disregarding the law of diminishing returns. Satisfying the interests and demands of Communist regimes can thus lead only to war, the course of which would be heavily determined in advance by the extent of our surrender prior to the failure of a policy of appeasement.

In all this, the internal situation and problems of Communist China must always be kept prominently in mind. With Hitler's Germany, foreign appeasement substantially strengthened the regime internally, solidified its internal support, and relegated the opposition to impotence and rejection. Today, as the Chinese Communists advance from one crisis to another, and as their solutions to problems become ever more radical and all-pervasive, any economic, political, or military concessions we may offer them in order to "alleviate tensions" or "normalize relations" will merely tend to weaken their growing internal opposition and make it more amenable to their control.

Today there seems little reason to doubt that the Chinese Communists are gradually but steadily working themselves into a problem of internal dissidence so massive that the mere slowness of its development may deceive us into unawareness of it. The impact of this dissidence will not likely be suddenly catastrophic like that of an avalanche. Rather it will probably be as slow, and irresistible, as the movement of a glacier. It is the task of a sophisticated economic and political warfare, backed up by constant military readiness, to aid and abet the development of massive dissidence among the suffering Chinese people.

Undoubtedly as this all goes on, there will develop numerous occasions on which there will erupt on the Chinese mainland explosions of dissidence large enough to tempt us to intervene. But toward all such our policy should be, while aiding and abetting them from the outside, not to intervene directly until Communist China is in veritable chaos. China is not Hungary, but if a sufficient explosion should occur to tempt the Russians in to help put it down, we can be sure that this will not be the last occasion of its kind. A stated unwillingness to intervene directly until and unless the finality of general chaos of the regime is secured, will do much to head off anything but the ultimate dissidence, namely a general and simultaneous rising in all parts of the country. The Chinese peasantry are quite as capable as is the Communist military leadership of using the "human sea" tactics.

But if all this is to be possible there are two major, and at the same time minimal, requirements: (1) the West, and particularly the United States cannot relax its hostility toward the Chinese Communist regime by concessions in either economic or political fields; and (2) our support of the Republic of China on Taiwan must be used as a positive weapon of political warfare against Communist China, with all that this implies in technical and personal implementation by us.

Finally, whatever our policy toward Communist China is to be, we must be prepared always for eventual war with it. Appeasement, on one extreme, will no doubt lead us into war with Communist China, as it did with Nazi Germany. On the other hand, a policy aimed at weakening the Communist regime from the inside may be less likely to result in the Communists choosing foreign war rather than internal breakup. But here the danger exists that, in anticipation of coming internal disaster to itself, the Chinese Communist regime may consider itself driven to a preventive foreign war. And no matter what middle ground we might try to seek between appeasement and outright opposition, the use of war by the Chinese Communists as a means of advancing their own interests cannot be eliminated. At all costs we must avoid seeking refuge in the "fact" that "rational people" could not possibly bring on a war with us on account of the "fact that they could not win," or the "fact that no one would win a nuclear war." Not even in the face of such "facts" as these would the Communists be likely to abandon their deeply rooted conviction that they can control the course of events, or that they need not fear to advance toward war since they can always, and in time, beat a strategic retreat if matters threaten to get "out of hand."

Thus, no matter how much we may abjure the use of force to settle the context between us, and no matter how much we may try to persuade the Chinese Communists to do the same thing, we must, even if we are resolved to avoid war "at any cost," always be prepared to use it as an instrument of national policy. This is the dangerous position we are now, as a minimum, forced to occupy, largely because when we could have contained Chinese Communism between 1945 and 1948, and eventually assisted in its destruction by military force, we refused to do so. Can anyone doubt that the extent of our militarization today, and the increasing necessity of our readiness for total war, have been magnified in a major way by our refusal between 1945 and 1948 to use such limited military measures as would then have been necessary to keep Chinese Communism under such a measure of repression as to eliminate it, effectively, as a factor in the world balance of power? Perhaps, after all, history *can* serve as a guide to present policy.

Part II

READINGS

TRADITIONAL CHINESE CONCEPTS OF LAW AND INTERNATIONAL SOCIETY[1]

The Chinese historian, Li Chien-nung, has given us (1948) a succinct statement of those aspects of traditional Chinese law and of the traditional pattern of China's relations with the outside world which lay at the basis of conflict with the Western powers during the nineteenth century. For many years the Westerners trading with China worked within the Chinese legal and diplomatic framework, while trying hard to secure changes. But after China's defeat in the Opium War the Western countries slowly achieved equality of treatment from the Chinese in diplomatic relations. And under a system of extraterritoriality their citizens in China were exempted from the application of Chinese law.

✓   ✓   ✓

Different Legal Conceptions

The direct causes of the Opium War were the seizure of foreign factories, the demand that foreign merchants sign a bond pledging not to sell opium, and the suspension of the supply of provisions to the British after the murder of Lin Wei-hsi. To the English there was a distinction between laws and orders. In their view, a government could not issue an order at random creating a new

[1] Li Chien-nung, *The Political History of China 1840-1928*, translated and edited by Ssu-yu Teng and Jeremy Ingalls (Princeton, 1956), pp. 45-46, 43-44.

crime. The responsibility for a given action could be borne only by the person in question, and not by other persons related in some way to him. Facts which formed a legal charge had, furthermore, to be supported by sufficient evidence. In addition, before it had been clearly established that a person had violated a law, he could not be stripped of personal liberty nor could his life be endangered.

Hence the British thought that the actions of Lin Tse-hsü were violent and unlawful. They considered that the bond which stated that if opium were smuggled, "the goods would be entirely confiscated by the government and the person responsible immediately executed" would make it possible to incriminate and execute a man without sufficient evidence. The seizing of factories and the cutting off of provisions were actions which, in the eyes of the Englishmen, were taken before the facts of responsibility had been definitely established. They held that these actions, carelessly placing the blame on all foreigners, deprived them of personal freedom and endangered their lives without due cause.

In contrast, under the autocratic government of the Chinese empire, the emperor's words were sacred; an imperial decree or instruction could become a new law. Officials with the seal of imperial commissioners . . . could "perform duties according to the exigency of the circumstances. . . ." In other words, the emperor was almost the only source of law. A new crime could be defined at any time either by his imperial decree or by his overt sanction or silent consent.

As to the problem of responsibility before the law, although there was a proverb, "A person who violates the law should be faced by himself alone," joint liability . . . was a customary legal practice to which there was no limit. Sometimes one person was involved; sometimes even the members of an entire clan were annihilated if the culprit could not be arrested. The leader of a community was held responsible for the actions of its members. The imperial decree condemned opium as an illicit traffic and Lin Tse-hsü as the imperial commissioner could perform his duty in any way he saw fit and effective, including the required signing of a bond. To lay siege to the foreign factories was to apply the principle of group responsibility "in order to eradicate the contraband commodity." In the opinion of the Chinese, since Elliot was the barbarian chief of England, he could bear group responsibility.

Once when the Hong merchants who had borrowed from foreigners were unable to pay their debts, the Chinese government had paid them from the official treasury. If Chinese authorities were responsible for the conduct of their merchants in China, why shouldn't the British barbarian chiefs be responsible for the activities of their subjects in China? In accord with this reasoning, Elliot was confined in the factories and was not permitted to leave until the British merchants surrendered their opium to the Chinese government. Since Lin Wei-hsi had been beaten to death by sailors from a British ship, the barbarian chief was blamed for not handing over the murderer to the Chinese authorities and for his failure to control the actions of his subordinates. To follow the precedent of 1808 by severing the supply of provisions to foreigners was, according to the reasoning of Chinese scholar-officials, a legitimate act.

These various concepts produced almost continuous conflicts until at last there was no alternative but war. The resultant Treaty of Nanking was a great shame and disgrace to China. Nevertheless, the roots of conflicts and conceptual differences still existed. At this time the Chinese still maintained that China was the source of civilization for the whole world, that the Western barbarians had no culture worth regarding, and that the power of Western guns was not a consequence of Western science. They took the recent defeat by the barbarians as merely an accident such as China had weathered many times in her long history. On the other hand, the Westerners recognized the inadequacies in this ancient Oriental nation. They assumed the knowledge and the techniques of Oriental peoples to be not much superior to those of African negroes or South Pacific islanders. "Oriental civilization" seemed to them merely an empty phrase. Aware of China's weaknesses, they extended their aggression step by step. China could no longer slumber. The Taiping Rebellion burst out; then the Anglo-French allies invaded Peking; and the imperial court was subjected to further rounds of insults.

Different Conceptions of International Society

The conception of an equal international society is fundamentally a product of modern history. In Europe it gradually developed after the Treaty of Westphalia in 1648. China, on the other hand, in ancient times had formed the conception that the entire world should be under the control of one emperor. During the periods called the Spring and Autumn [722-482 B.C.] and the Warring States [481-221 B.C.], the numerous feudal lords were independent under conditions resembling those of modern European international societies. However, above all the feudal lords was the figurehead of the Emperor of the Chou dynasty [ca. 1100-221 B.C.]. Mencius quoted Confucius as saying, "In the sky there is no more than one sun, and above the people there is no more than one emperor." After Ch'in Shih-huang-ti unified China [221 B.C.] the conception of having a large, self-sufficient empire controlled by one royal family was even more firmly implanted, and the conception has been maintained ever since.

The ideal empire was demarcated by a line which separated the Chinese from the barbarians. . . . Boundary lines between Chinese and barbarians were gradually expanded. . . . This was the world-nation conception of the Chinese as well as their conception of international society; the tradition handed down for millennia and was reinforced by the Ch'in and Han dynasties.

Because this conception was deeply rooted in the minds of the Chinese people, they regarded all special envoys sent by Western nations as tribute-bearers. They flatly rejected the suggestion that they exchange ministers as well as maintain diplomatic intercourse on an equal footing with other nations. In the long history of China, foreigners have seldom been regarded as equals. The marriage of the women of the Han dynasty to the barbarian Hsiung-nu, for example, and the treaty which made the Sung rulers and the Khitan "brothers" were taken as great humiliations. How could the Chinese be expected to lower their pride and dignity before people with blue eyes and red beards, or easily break down the old boundaries between themselves and barbarians? On the other hand, in Europe after the Treaty of Westphalia, even a tiny state enjoyed its status of equality in international society. Hence, how could England, which had vast overseas possessions, be willing to take insults from the Chinese government?

— Reading No. 2 —

TREATY OF NANKING, AUGUST 29, 1842[2]

This treaty opened China to foreign residence and trade. Other Western powers soon secured by treaty the rights in China thus extracted by Britain as a result of the Opium War. The Chinese ports opened to trade became known as "treaty ports," and the privileges gained in the treaties were commonly referred to as "treaty rights." All these agreements were commonly termed by the Chinese the "unequal treaties" on account of the derogations from Chinese sovereignty which they contained, especially the control by foreign powers over Chinese tariff rates and the exemptions of foreign nationals from the jurisdiction of Chinese law.

↗   ↗   ↗

ARTICLE I. There shall henceforward be Peace and Friendship between Her Majesty the Queen of the United Kingdom of Great Britain and Ireland, and His Majesty the Emperor of China, and between their respective Subjects, who shall enjoy full security and protection for their persons and property within the Dominions of the other.

ARTICLE II. His Majesty the Emperor of China agrees

---

[2] The Maritime Customs, *Treaties, Conventions, etc., between China and Foreign States* (2nd ed., Shanghai, 1917), Vol. I, pp. 351-356.

that British Subjects, with their families and establishments, shall be allowed to reside, for the purpose of carrying on their Mercantile pursuits, without molestation or restraint at the Cities and Towns of Canton, Amoy, Foochow-fu, Ningpo, and Shanghai, and Her Majesty the Queen of Great Britain, etc., will appoint Superintendents or Consular Officers, to reside at each of the above-named Cities or Towns, to be the medium of communication between the Chinese Authorities and the said Merchants, and to see that the just Duties and other Dues of the Chinese Government as hereafter provided for, are duly discharged by Her Britannic Majesty's Subjects.

ARTICLE III. It being obviously necessary and desirable, that British Subjects should have some Port whereat they may careen and refit their Ships, when required, and keep Stores for that purpose, His Majesty the Emperor of China cedes to Her Majesty the Queen of Great Britain, etc., the Island of Hongkong, to be possessed in perpetuity by Her Britannic Majesty, Her Heirs and Successors, and to be governed by such Laws and Regulations as Her Majesty the Queen of Great Britain, etc., shall see fit to direct.

ARTICLE IV. The Emperor of China agrees to pay the sum of Six Millions of Dollars as the value of Opium which was delivered up at Canton in the month of March 1839, as a Ransom for the lives of Her Britannic Majesty's Superintendent and Subjects, who had been imprisoned and threatened with death by the Chinese High Officers.

ARTICLE V. The Government of China having compelled the British Merchants trading at Canton to deal exclusively with certain Chinese Merchants called Hong Merchants (or Cohong) who had been licensed by the Chinese Government for that purpose, the Emperor of China agrees to abolish that practice in future at all Ports where British Merchants may reside, and to permit them to carry on their mercantile transactions with whatever persons they please, and His Imperial Majesty further agrees to pay to the British Government the sum of Three Millions of Dollars, on account of Debts due to British Subjects by some of the said Hong Merchants (or Cohong), who have become insolvent, and who owe very large sums of money to Subjects of Her Britannic Majesty.

ARTICLE VI. The Government of Her Britannic Majesty having been obliged to send out an Expedition to demand and obtain redress for the violent and unjust Proceedings of the Chinese High Authorities towards Her Britannic Majesty's Officer and Subjects, the Emperor of China agrees to pay the sum of Twelve Millions of Dollars on account of the Expenses incurred, and Her Britannic Majesty's Plenipotentiary voluntarily agrees, on behalf of Her Majesty, to deduct from the said amount of Twelve Millions of Dollars, any sums which may have been received by Her Majesty's combined Forces as Ransom for Cities and Towns in China, subsequent to the 1st day of August 1841.

ARTICLE VII. It is agreed that the Total amount of Twenty-one Millions of Dollars, described in the three preceding Articles, shall be paid as follows:—

Six Millions immediately.

Six Millions in 1843. That is:— Three Millions on or before the 30th of the month of June, and Three Millions on or before the 31st of December.

Five Millions in 1844. That is:— Two Millions and a Half on or before the 30th of June, and Two Millions and a Half on or before the 31st of December.

Four Millions in 1845. That is:— Two Millions on or before the 30th of June, and Two Millions on or before the 31st of December; and it is further stipulated, that Interest at the rate of 5 per cent. per annum, shall be paid by the Government of China on any portions of the above sums that are not punctually discharged at the periods fixed.

ARTICLE VIII. The Emperor of China agrees to release unconditionally all Subjects of Her Britannic Majesty (whether Natives of Europe or India) who may be in confinement at this moment, in any part of the Chinese Empire.

ARTICLE IX. The Emperor of China agrees to publish and promulgate, under His Imperial Sign Manual and Seal, a full and entire amnesty and act of indemnity, to all Subjects of China on account of their having resided under, or having had dealings and intercourse with, or having entered the Service of Her Britannic Majesty, or of Her Majesty's officers, and His Imperial Majesty further engages to release all Chinese Subjects who may be at this moment in confinement for similar reasons.

ARTICLE X. His Majesty the Emperor of China agrees to establish at all the Ports which are by the 2nd article of this Treaty to be thrown open for the resort of British Merchants, a fair and regular Tariff of Export and Import Customs and other Dues, which Tariff shall be publicly notified and promulgated for general information, and the Emperor further engages, that when British Merchandise shall have once paid at any of the said Ports the regulated Customs and Dues agreeable to the Tariff, to be hereafter fixed, such Merchandise may be conveyed by Chinese Merchants, to any Province or City in the interior of the Empire of China on paying a further amount as Transit Duties which shall not exceed [blank] per cent. on the tariff value of such goods.

ARTICLE XI. It is agreed that Her Britannic Majesty's Chief High Officer in China shall correspond with the Chinese High Officers, both at the Capital and in the Provinces, under the term "Communication." . . . The Subordinate British Officers and Chinese High Officers in the Provinces under the terms "Statement" . . . on the part of the former, and on the part of the latter, "Declaration," . . . and the Subordinates of both Countries on a footing of perfect equality. Merchants and others not holding official situations and, therefore, not included in the above, on both sides, to use the term "Representation" . . . in all Papers addressed to, or intended for the notice of the respective Governments.

ARTICLE XII. On the assent of the Emperor of China to this Treaty being received and the discharge of the first instalment of money, Her Britannic Majesty's Forces will retire from Nanking and the Grand Canal, and will no longer molest or stop the Trade of China. The Military Post at Chinhai will also be withdrawn, but the Islands of Koolangsoo and that of Chusan will continue to be held by Her Majesty's Forces until the money payments, and the arrangements for opening the Ports to British Merchants be completed.

ARTICLE XIII. The Ratification of this Treaty by Her Majesty the Queen of Great Britain, etc., and His Majesty the Emperor of China shall be exchanged as soon as the great distance which separates England from China will admit; but in the meantime counterpart copies of it, signed and sealed by the Plenipotentiaries on behalf of their respective Sovereigns, shall be mutually delivered, and all its provisions and arrangements shall take effect.

Done at Nanking, and Signed and Sealed by the Plenipotentiaries on board Her Britannic Majesty's ship *Cornwallis*, this twenty-ninth day of August, 1842, corresponding with the Chinese date, twenty-fourth day of the seventh month in the twenty-second Year of Taou Kwang.

— Reading No. 3 —

THE "BURLINGAME" TREATY, JULY 28, 1868[3]

The first American treaty with China, 1844, was followed by numerous others which further developed the relations between the two countries. The so-called "Burlingame" Treaty, after the American of that name who represented the Emperor of China on missions to various world capitals, is notable for the general mutuality of its provisions, especially those relating to diplomatic representation and to residence, travel, and freedom of religious practice of nationals of each signatory in the territory of the other.

   ✓   ✓   ✓

ARTICLE I. His Majesty the Emperor of China being of the opinion that in making concessions to the citizens

[3] The Maritime Customs, *Treaties, Conventions, etc., between China and Foreign States* (2nd ed., Shanghai, 1917), Vol. I, pp. 729-734.

or subjects of Foreign powers of the privilege of residing on certain tracts of land or resorting to certain waters of that Empire for purposes of trade, he has by no means relinquished his right of eminent domain or dominion over the said lands and waters, hereby agrees that no such concession or grant shall be construed to give any power or party which may be at war with or hostile to the United States the right to attack the citizens of the United States or their property within the said lands or waters; and the United States, for themselves, hereby agree to abstain from offensively attacking the citizens or subjects of any power or party, or their property, with which they may be at war on any such tract of land or waters of the said Empire. But nothing in this Article shall be construed to prevent the United States from resisting an attack by any hostile power or party upon their citizens or their property.

It is further agreed that if any right or interest in any tract of land in China has been or shall hereafter be granted by the Government of China to the United States or their citizens for purposes of trade or commerce, that grant shall in no event be construed to divest the Chinese authorities of their right of jurisdiction over persons and property within said tract of land, except so far as the right may have been expressly relinquished by Treaty.

ARTICLE II. The United States of America and His Majesty the Emperor of China, believing that the safety and prosperity of commerce will thereby best be promoted, agree that any privilege or immunity in respect to trade or navigation within the Chinese dominions which may not have been stipulated for by Treaty shall be subject to the discretion of the Chinese Government, and may be regulated by it accordingly, but not in a manner or spirit incompatible with the Treaty stipulations of the parties.

ARTICLE III. The Emperor of China shall have the right to appoint Consuls at ports of the United States, who shall enjoy the same privileges and immunities as those which are enjoyed by public law and Treaty in the United States by the Consuls of Great Britain and Russia, or either of them.

ARTICLE IV. The 29th Article of the Treaty of the 18th

of June 1858 having stipulated for the exemption of
Christian citizens of the United States and Chinese converts from persecution in China on account of their
faith, it is further agreed that citizens of the United
States in China of every religious persuasion, and Chinese subjects in the United States, shall enjoy entire
liberty of conscience, and shall be exempt from all dis-
ability or persecution on account of their religious faith
or worship in either country. Cemeteries for sepulture of
the dead, of whatever nativity or nationality, shall be
held in respect and free from disturbance or profanation.

ARTICLE V. The United States of America and the
Emperor of China cordially recognise the inherent and
inalienable right of man to change his home and allegiance, and also the mutual advantage of the free migration and emigration of their citizens and subjects respectively from the one country to the other, for the purposes
of curiosity, of trade, or as permanent residents. The
high contracting parties therefore join in reprobating any
other than an entirely voluntary emigration for these purposes. They consequently agree to pass laws making it a
penal offence for a citizen of the United States or Chinese subjects to take Chinese subjects either to the
United States or to any other Foreign country, or for a
Chinese subject or citizen of the United States to take
citizens of the United States to China or to any other
Foreign country, without their free and voluntary consent respectively.

ARTICLE VI. Citizens of the United States visiting or
residing in China shall enjoy the same privileges, immunities, or exemptions in respect to travel or residence as
may there be enjoyed by the citizens or subjects of the
most favoured nation; and, reciprocally, Chinese subjects
visiting or residing in the United States shall enjoy the
same privileges, immunities, and exemptions in respect
to travel or residence as may there be enjoyed by the
citizens or subjects of the most favoured nation. But
nothing herein contained shall be held to confer naturali-
sations upon citizens of the United States in China, nor
upon the subjects of China in the United States.

ARTICLE VII. Citizens of the United States shall enjoy
all the privileges of the public educational institutions
under the control of the Government of China, and,

reciprocally, Chinese subjects shall enjoy all the privileges of the public educational institutions under the control of the Government of the United States, which are enjoyed in the respective countries by the citizens or subjects of the most favoured nation. The citizens of the United States may freely establish and maintain schools within the Empire of China at those places where Foreigners are by Treaty permitted to reside; and, reciprocally, the Chinese subjects may enjoy the same privileges and immunities in the United States. . . .

— Reading No. 4 —

CHINESE EXCLUSION ACTS OF MAY 6, 1882 AND MAY 5, 1892[4]

At the same time as the United States, together with the other powers, was pressing China for the expansion of her rights in China, she was acting to limit strictly the coming to the United States of Chinese citizens. Laws passed by Congress to do this were directly contrary to treaties with China. (See Reading No. 3.) But they were upheld in the courts, and ultimately the treaties were revised along this line. But there was no corresponding impairment of the right of Americans freely to go to

[4] An act to execute certain treaty stipulations relating to Chinese, *The Statutes at Large of the United States of America, from December, 1881, to March, 1883* . . . (Washington, 1883), Vol. XXII, p. 58-61; an act to prohibit the coming of Chinese persons into the United States, *The Statutes at Large of the United States of America, from December, 1891, to March, 1893* . . . (Washington, 1893), Vol. XXVII, pp. 25-26.

China. Such a form of inequality and unilateralism was possible only because the Chinese Empire was weak and unable to resist the foreign powers.

✓   ✓   ✓

Whereas, in the opinion of the Government of the United States the coming of Chinese laborers to this country endangers the good order of certain localities within the territory thereof: Therefore,

Be it enacted by the Senate and House of Representatives of the United States of America in Congress assembled, That from and after the expiration of ninety days next after the passage of this act, and until the expiration of ten years next after the passage of this act, the coming of Chinese laborers to the United States be, and the same is hereby, suspended; and during such suspension it shall not be lawful for any Chinese laborer to come, or, having so come after the expiration of said ninety days, to remain within the United States. . . .

SEC. 13. That this act shall not apply to diplomatic and other officers of the Chinese Government traveling upon the business of that government, whose credentials shall be taken as equivalent to the certificate in this act mentioned, and shall exempt them and their body and household servants from the provisions of this act as to other Chinese persons.

SEC. 14. That hereafter no State court or court of the United States shall admit Chinese to citizenship; and all laws in conflict with this act are hereby repealed.

SEC. 15. That the words "Chinese laborers," wherever used in this act, shall be construed to mean both skilled and unskilled laborers and Chinese employed in mining.

Approved, May 6, 1882.

Be it enacted by the Senate and House of Representatives of the United States of America in Congress assembled, That all laws now in force prohibiting and regulating the coming into this country of Chinese persons and persons of Chinese descent are hereby continued in force for a period of ten years from the passage of this act.

SEC. 2. That any Chinese person or person of Chinese descent, when convicted and adjudged under any of said laws to be not lawfully entitled to be or remain in the

United States, shall be removed from the United States to China, unless he or they shall make it appear to the justice, judge, or commissioner before whom he or they are tried that he or they are subjects or citizens of some other country, in which case he or they shall be removed from the United States to such country: *Provided,* That in any case where such other country of which such Chinese person shall claim to be a citizen or subject shall demand any tax as a condition of the removal of such person to that country, he or she shall be removed to China.

SEC. 3. That any Chinese person of Chinese descent arrested under the provisions of this act or the acts hereby extended shall be adjudged to be unlawfully within the United States unless such person shall establish, by affirmative proof, to the satisfaction of such justice, judge, or commissioner, his lawful right to remain in the United States.

SEC. 4. That any such Chinese person or person of Chinese descent convicted and adjudged to be not lawfully entitled to be or remain in the United States shall be imprisoned at hard labor for a period of not exceeding one year and thereafter removed from the United States, as hereinafter provided.

SEC. 5. That after the passage of this act on application to any judge or court of the United States in the first instance for a writ of habeas corpus, by a Chinese person seeking to land in the United States, to whom that privilege has been denied, no bail shall be allowed, and such application shall be heard and determined promptly without unnecessary delay.

SEC. 6. And it shall be the duty of all Chinese laborers within the limits of the United States, at the time of the passage of this act, and who are entitled to remain in the United States, to apply to the collector of internal revenue of their respective districts, within one year after the passage of this act, for a certificate of residence, and any Chinese laborer, within the limits of the United States, who shall neglect, fail, or refuse to comply with the provisions of this act, or who, after one year from the passage hereof, shall be found within the jurisdiction of the United States without such certificate of residence, shall be deemed and adjudged to be unlawfully within the United States, and may be arrested, by any United States customs official, collector of internal revenue or his deputies, United States marshal or his deputies, and taken before a United States judge, whose duty it shall be to order that he be deported from the United States as hereinbefore provided, unless he shall establish clearly to the satisfaction of said judge, that by reason of accident, sickness or other unavoidable cause, he has been unable to procure his certificate, and to the satisfaction of the court, and by at least one credible white witness, that he was a resident of the United States at the time of the passage of this act; and if upon the hearing, it shall appear that he is so entitled to a certificate, it shall be granted upon his paying the cost. Should it appear that said Chinaman had procured a certificate which has been lost or destroyed, he shall be detained and judgment suspended a reasonable time to enable him to procure a duplicate from the officer granting it, and in such cases, the cost of said arrest and trial shall be in the discretion of the court. And any Chinese person other than a Chinese laborer, having a right to be and remain in the United States, desiring such certificate as evidence of such right may apply for and receive the same without charge. . . .

Approved, May 5, 1892

— Reading No. 5 —

VICEROY CHANG CHIH-TUNG ON HOW TO SAVE CHINA, 1898 [5]

Chang Chih-tung's famous essay was a reaction from China's defeat by Japan (1894-1895) and the consequent

[5] Chang Chih-tung, *"Learn!"*, trans. by S. I. Woodbridge (Shanghai, n.d.), pp. 8, 9, 13-14, 31-33, 40-42, 48-42, 48-50, 60-61.

threat of China's breakup at the hands of the powers. Reformers seized upon it, and the Emperor had it widely distributed. Chang's purpose was to advocate gradual change, using education to foster a revived Confucianism along with Western technology. Thus, he hoped, the traditional culture of China could be preserved and the dynasty maintained in power by providing China with the protection of economic and military strength on the Western model.

✓   ✓   ✓

In no period of China's history has there arisen an emergency like the present. It is a time of change, and His Imperial Highness, the Emperor of China, has accepted the situation by altering somewhat the system of civil and military examinations and by establishing schools. New plans are being formed for the welfare of the country by Chinese philanthropists, but these plans differ both in degree and kind. . . .

The present condition of things is not due to outside nations, but to China herself. It has ever been true that the number of our able men has been proportioned to the good qualities of the government, and that morals are gauged by the conduct of the schools. In view of many facts, and with the hope of relieving my country from her present embarrassments, I, the Viceroy of the Liang Hu, have prepared this work especially for the Chinese under my jurisdiction, and generally for my countrymen in the other provinces. . . .

We would here state that there are now three things necessary to be done in order to save China from revolution. The first is to maintain the reigning dynasty; the second is to conserve the holy religion; and the third is to protect the Chinese race. These are inseparably connected; in fact they together constitute one; for in order to protect the Chinese race we must first conserve the religion, and if the religion is to be conserved we are bound to maintain the dynasty. But, it may be asked, how can we protect the race? We reply, by knowledge; and knowledge is religion; and religion is propagated by strength; and strength lies in the troops. Consequently in countries of no prestige and power the native religion is not followed, and in kingdoms that are not prosperous the native race is held in light esteem by their more fortunate neighbors. Mohammedanism is unreasonable, but Turkey is fierce and warlike, so Mohammedanism survives. Buddhism is near the truth, but India is stupid and foolish, and Buddhism perishes. Nestorionism waned because Persia grew weak, and the old Greek religion flickers for the same reason. Roman Catholicism and Protestantism have been propagated over three-fifths of the globe by the power of the military.

Our holy religion has flourished in China several thousand years without change. The early Emperors and Kings embellished our tenets by their noble examples and bequeathed to us the rich legacy which we now possess. The sovereigns were the teachers. . . . The Emperors themselves follow the truth and then instruct all in the empire, so that every one that has breath knows how to honour and how to love. For government and religion are inseparably linked together and constitute the warp of the past and present, the purport of intercommunication between China and the West. . . .

In order to render China powerful, and at the same time preserve our own institutions, it is absolutely necessary that we should utilize Western knowledge. But unless Chinese learning is made the basis of education, and a Chinese direction given to thought, the strong will become anarchists, and the weak slaves. Thus, the latter end will be worse than the former. The English newspapers have recently been ridiculing us for not reforming, and they state that the teachings of Confucius lie at the bottom of our inflexible conservatism. In this they are greatly mistaken. Those who have translated the Four Books and Five Classics into foreign languages, have missed the true intent of Confucianism by accepting the explanations of inefficient Chinese teachers who knew nothing whatever of our doctrine. These newspapers get their information from these translated books, and ridicule what they know nothing about. The superficial Chinese commentaries which pass current for truth, the unconnected, non-cohesive eight-legged essays, the effete philosophies, countless antiquarian works, false but high-sounding poetry of China, are not Confucian learning. And the stereotyped rules of deportment which are prescribed by the "master of ceremonies," and followed by

Chinese officials, are heresies from the school of Han Fei and Li Sh, which had their origin in the stormy times of Ts'in. The vulgar herd of Chinese officials who observe these forms, make a virtue of obstructiveness and cloak their laziness in matters of vital importance by "quieting the people," as it is called. On the ground of "nourishing the constitution of the state," they continue their malpractices; and it is said that these constitute the Confucian government! We characterize this system as the teaching of Lao Tsz, the tail-ends of previous dynasties, and the devices by which slippery officials carry on their trade. Emphatically, it is not that mode of government recommended by our great sage.

Confucian learning consists in the acquisition of extensive literature and the strict observance of what is right; in the profound and careful meditation of the old in order to understand the new; in the making of one's self the peer of heaven by means of perfect sincerity and thus influencing men in all things for good.

Confucian government consists in rendering honour to whom honour is due, and filial piety to whom filial piety is due; in first providing a sufficiency for the people, and afterwards instructing them; in preparing for war in time of peace, and in doing things at the proper time and in the proper manner. Confucius is equal to the thousand sages and the hundred kings. He is the co-equal and the co-worker with heaven and earth in nourishing and transforming men and things. How, then, can it be said that he is like the effete and inoperative "scholar" of today . . . ?

Our scholars to-day should become conversant with the classics, in order to understand the real intent of the early sages and philosophers in establishing our religion; and a knowledge of history should be acquired in order to become familiar with our Chinese governmental methods and customs in past generations. The literary relics of our schoolmen should be gone over, to profit withal, in learning and literature. After this is done, our deficiency in books can be supplied from Western sources, and our government ills be cured by Western physicians. In this way, China can derive benefit from foreign countries, without incurring the danger of adopting Western methods that would be prejudicial to her best interests. . . . In Western educational institutions a daily study of the Bible is compulsory. This shows a respect for the Christian religion. The students in the lower schools first learn Latin in order to preserve what is ancient; and in order to observe the proper sequence of things, a thorough knowledge of the country's geography and a general acquaintance with that of other countries is required. The literature of their schools extols the excellence of their ancient Emperors' governments; and both in public and private the notes of their music swell forth in praise of the bravery and prosperity of the fatherland. These things manifest the patriotism of Western people. . . . Without a basis of native literature the Chinese who acquires this Western learning, will loathe his country in proportion as his scientific knowledge increases; and although his knowledge may be perfected to a high degree, how can our country employ him if he does not know Chinese? . . .

China received her first warning in Formosa when the aborigines rebelled, the second in the Liu Ch'ieu Islands, the third in Ili, the fourth in Korea, the fifth in Annam and Burmah, and the sixth in the Japanese war, and the country is now in extreme danger. The warnings have been sent by Heaven to open the eyes of the Chinese, and the Chinese officials and people elect to remain blind, stubborn, and proud as of old. What more can we say?

At the present time it is imperative that Chinese rulers should be thoroughly versed in governmental policy, laws, political economy, commerce, etc.; that the farmer should know about the selection of seeds, the adaptation of soil, farming implements and fertilizers; that the workman should be skilled in the use of the best tools and the selection of materials; that the merchant should seek to discover new lands, to manufacture new goods, and to become acquainted with the state of the markets both at home and abroad; and that the soldier should become familiar with ships, arms, forts, batteries, target-practice, and other subjects. . . . But China still observes the "old custom" along these lines, and is not willing to strive after something useful, because it is novel, and if we do not change soon, what will become of us? European knowledge will increase more and more, and Chinese stupidity will become more dense. We shall be marked as the sure prey of the West; foreigners will still trade with us as before, but China will play a losing game, and get only chaff whilst her competitors garner the wheat, and we shall really, if not openly, become the slaves of Westerners. Not only this, the foreigners will suck our blood and, worse than this, pare the flesh from our bones. To end the tragedy they will swallow us down, body and soul, at one great gulp, and gloat over the deed!

Knowledge alone can save us from destruction, and the literati ought to take the lead in the matter and instruct the farmer, the workman, the merchant, and the soldier in their different spheres; but if the educated class remains ignorant how can this be done? . . .

How shall we obtain knowledge? First, putting away all that is . . . stubbornness, empty form and pride. Secondly, we must get rid of . . . our slipshod, drifting habit of depending upon mere fortuity for success. Unless we free ourselves from these, all that is left for the Chinese is to become

"Like dumb, driven cattle,"

or like the grass that is trodden down by him. . . .

In establishing these schools there are five important factors.

First.—The old and new must both be taught; by the old is meant the Four Books, the Five Classics, history, government and geography of China; by the new, Western government, science and history. Both are imperative, but we repeat that the old is to form the basis and the new is for practical purposes.

Second.—The comparative study of governments and science, colleges, geography, political economy, customs, taxes, military regulations, laws, and expositions come under the head of Western government. Mathematics, mining, therapeutics, sound, light, chemistry, and electricity are classed under Western science. . . . On the whole, a knowledge of government is more necessary than a knowledge of science if we are to save the country; but the student of government should acquire some knowledge of science in order to carry on the government.

Third.—We must teach the young. Let the course of study be adapted to the qualifications of the student. Pupils with bright minds should learn mathematics; those with good perspective sense, drawing; those with inventive powers, mechanics, chemistry and manufactures; those with a clear pronunciation, languages; and those of robust frame, athletics. It will be difficult for men of middle age and above to take a thorough course.

Fourth.—Abolish the eight-legged essay. Let the new learning be the test of scholarship, but include the classics, history, geography, and government of China in the examinations. The true essay will then come out. If so desired, the eight-legged essays can be studied at home; but why bother the school with them and at the same time waste time and strength that can be expended in something more profitable?

Fifth.—Abolish the scramble for money. Students in foreign institutions are required to pay their own board and tuition. Salaries are never paid to them. The custom of paying the students, which obtains in our Chinese schools, was originally good in the intention to aid the indigent. It was, however, mistaken policy, for many students now come merely for the loaves and fishes and create a deal of trouble if their demands are not satisfied. . . . Thus an originally good principle has been abused by sordid motives. . . .

In this dynasty there have been many innovations introduced in spite of opposition. The men who stoutly resisted the introduction of steamboats and railways would now be the very first to resist their abolishment.

The anti-reformers may be roughly divided into three classes:—

First, the moss-backs, who are stuck in the mud of antiquity. . . .

Second, the slow bellies of Chinese officialdom, who in case of reform would be compelled to bestir themselves, and who would be held responsible for the outlay of money and men necessary for the changes. The secret machinations of these befuddled, indolent, slippery nepotists thwart all schemes of reform. . . .

Third, the hypercritics.

— Reading No. 6 —

THE OPEN DOOR POLICY, SEPTEMBER 6, 1899[6]

In his note to the American Ambassador in Great Britain, Secretary of State John Hay moved to secure official British approval for an attempt at preventing the "spheres of influence" of the various powers in China from developing into exclusive colonial possessions. The open door, that is, equal access for all to trade, was a deeply rooted feature of American Far Eastern policy. It had been embodied in the most-favored-nation provision of our treaty with Siam as early as 1833, and such provisions were included in the treaties of the powers with China. The Hay initiative in support of it in 1899 had developed with Britain's help and approval, but was met with little enthusiasm by the other powers, most of whom looked forward to the breakup of China which they considered imminent at that time.

✓   ✓   ✓

Sir: The Government of Her Britannic Majesty has declared that its policy and its very traditions precluded it from using any privileges which might be granted it in China as a weapon for excluding commercial rivals, and that freedom of trade for Great Britain in that Empire meant freedom of trade for all the world alike. While conceding by formal agreements, first with Germany and then with Russia, the possession of "spheres of influence or interest" in China in which they are to enjoy special rights and privileges, more especially in respect of railroads and mining enterprises, Her Britannic Majesty's

[6] *United States Relations with China with Special Reference to the Period 1944-1949* (Released August 1949, Division of Publication, Office of Public Affairs, Dept. of State), pp. 414-416.

Government has therefore sought to maintain at the same time what is called the "open-door" policy, to insure to the commerce of the world in China equality of treatment within said "spheres" for commerce and navigation. This latter policy is alike urgently demanded by the British mercantile communities and by those of the United States, as it is justly held by them to be the only one which will improve existing conditions, enable them to maintain their positions in the markets of China, and extend their operations in the future. While the Government of the United States will in no way commit itself to a recognition of exclusive rights of any power within or control over any portion of the Chinese Empire under such agreements as have within the last year been made, it cannot conceal its apprehension that under existing conditions there is a possibility, even a probability, of complications arising between the treaty powers which may imperil the rights insured to the United States under our treaties with China.

This Government is animated by a sincere desire that the interests of our citizens may not be prejudiced through exclusive treatment by any of the controlling powers within their so-called "spheres of interest" in China, and hopes also to retain there an open market for the commerce of the world, remove dangerous sources of international irritation, and hasten thereby united or concerted action of the powers at Pekin in favor of the administrative reforms so urgently needed for strengthening the Imperial Government and maintaining the integrity of China in which the whole western world is alike concerned. It believes that such a result may be greatly assisted by a declaration by the various powers claiming "spheres of interest" in China of their intentions as regards treatment of foreign trade therein. The present moment seems a particularly opportune one for informing Her Britannic Majesty's Government of the desire of the United States to see it make a formal declaration and to lend its support in obtaining similar declarations from the various powers claiming "spheres of influence" in China, to the effect that each in its respective spheres of interest or influence

First. Will in no wise interfere with any treaty port or

any vested interest within any so-called "sphere of interest" or leased territory it may have in China.

Second. That the Chinese treaty tariff of the time
being shall apply to all merchandise landed or shipped
to all such ports as are within said "sphere of interest"
(unless they be "free ports"), no matter to what nationality it may belong, and that duties so leviable shall be col-
lected by the Chinese Government.

Third. That it will levy no higher harbor duties on
vessels of another nationality frequenting any port in
such "sphere" than shall be levied on vessels of its own
nationality, and no higher railroad charges over lines
built, controlled, or operated within its "sphere" on
merchandise belonging to citizens or subjects of other
nationalities transported through such "sphere" than shall
be levied on similar merchandise belonging to its own
nationals transported over equal distances. . . .

You will, at as early date as practicable, submit the
considerations to Her Britannic Majesty's principal secretary of state for foreign affairs and request their immediate consideration. . . .

— Reading No. 7 —

THE NINE-POWER TREATY,
FEBRUARY 6, 1922[7]

*This treaty illustrates the weakness of international
agreements in the absence of effective sanctions against
their violation. Designed to head off the threat that Japan
would make China into a protectorate of Nippon, it*

[7] *United States Relations with China with Special Reference to
the Period 1944-1949* (Released August 1949, Division
of Publication, Office of Public Affairs, Dept. of State),
pp. 438-442.

eventually failed to do so when Japan seized Manchuria in 1931 and went on into North China. In such a case of treaty violation all that was provided for in the pact was "full and frank communication" between the signatories. The powers had failed to place behind the treaty a commitment to use force to uphold it, and thus Japan successfully nullified it. This illustrates the simple truth that a nation cannot attempt to avoid war over an issue unless, paradoxically, it is able and willing to employ force as a sanction to uphold agreements made in the hope of peace.

✓   ✓   ✓

The United States of America, Belgium, the British Empire, China, France, Italy, Japan, the Netherlands and Portugal:

Desiring to adopt a policy designed to stabilize conditions in the Far East, to safeguard the rights and interests of China, and to promote intercourse between China and the other Powers upon the basis of equality of opportunity;

Have resolved to conclude a treaty for that purpose. . . .

ARTICLE I. The Contracting Powers, other than China, agree:

(1) To respect the sovereignty, the independence, and the territorial and administrative integrity of China;

(2) To provide the fullest and most unembarrassed opportunity to China to develop and maintain for herself an effective and stable government;

(3) To use their influence for the purpose of effectually establishing and maintaining the principle of equal opportunity for the commerce and industry of all nations throughout the territory of China;

(4) To refrain from taking advantage of conditions in China in order to seek special rights or privileges which would abridge the rights of subjects or citizens of friendly States, and from countenancing action inimical to the security of such States.

ARTICLE II. The Contracting Powers agree not to enter into any treaty, agreement, arrangement, or understanding, either with one another, or, individually or collectively, with any Power or Powers, which would infringe or impair the principles stated in Article I.

ARTICLE III. With a view to applying more effectually the principles of the Open Door or equality of opportunity in China for the trade and industry of all nations, the Contracting Powers, other than China, agree that they will not seek, nor support their respective nationals in seeking—

(a) any arrangement which might purport to establish in favour of their interests any general superiority of rights with respect to commercial or economic development in any designated region of China;

(b) any such monopoly or preference as would deprive the nationals of any other Power of the right of undertaking any legitimate trade or industry in China, or of participating with the Chinese Government, or with any local authority, in any category of public enterprise, or which by reason of its scope, duration or geographical extent is calculated to frustrate the practical application of the principle of equal opportunity.

It is understood that the foregoing stipulations of this Article are not to be so construed as to prohibit the acquisition of such properties or rights as may be necessary to the conduct of a particular commercial, industrial, or financial undertaking or to the encouragement of invention and research.

China undertakes to be guided by the principles stated in the foregoing stipulations of this Article in dealing with applications for economic rights and privileges from Governments and nationals of all foreign countries, whether parties to the present Treaty or not.

ARTICLE IV. The Contracting Powers agree not to support any agreements by their respective nationals with each other designed to create Spheres of Influence or to provide for the enjoyment of mutually exclusive opportunities in designated parts of Chinese territory.

ARTICLE V. China agrees that, throughout the whole of the railways in China, she will not exercise or permit unfair discrimination of any kind. In particular there shall be no discrimination whatever, direct or indirect, in respect of charges or of facilities on the ground of the nationality of passengers or the countries from which or to which they are proceeding, or the origin or ownership of goods or the country from which or to which they are consigned, or the nationality or ownership of the ship or other means of conveying such passengers or goods before or after their transport on the Chinese Railways.

The Contracting Powers, other than China, assume a corresponding obligation in respect of any of the aforesaid railways over which they or their nationals are in a position to exercise any control in virtue of any concession, special agreement or otherwise.

ARTICLE VI. The Contracting Powers, other than China, agree fully to respect China's rights as a neutral in time of war to which China is not a party; and China declares that when she is a neutral she will observe the obligations of neutrality.

ARTICLE VII. The Contracting Powers agree that, whenever a situation arises which in the opinion of any one of them involves the application of the stipulations of the present Treaty, and renders desirable discussion of such application, there shall be full and frank communication between the Contracting Powers concerned.

ARTICLE VIII. Powers not signatory to the present Treaty, which have Governments recognized by the Signatory Powers and which have treaty relations with China, shall be invited to adhere to the present Treaty. To this end the Government of the United States will make the necessary communications to nonsignatory Powers and will inform the Contracting Powers of the replies received. Adherence by any Power shall become effective on receipt of notice thereof by the Government of the United States. . . .

— Reading No. 8 —

SUMMARY OF THE *SAN MIN CHU I*[8]

The Three People's Principles (San Min Chu I) *of Dr. Sun Yat-sen comprise the official ideology of the Kuomin-*

[8] *China Yearbook, 1957-58* (Taipei, 1958), pp. 50-51.

tang (*The Nationalist Party of China*). *They have become as fundamental to the revolution which Dr. Sun headed in China as the Declaration of Independence was to the American Revolution. Wherever the Kuomintang has held sway, Dr. Sun's ideas have been effectively promulgated through every possible medium. They are studied in all schools. This short summary is from an official source.*

✓   ✓   ✓

The Three People's Principles have guided the building of the nation: they are also the principles to be observed by the Kuomintang. They are Nationalism, Democracy, and People's Livelihood, an integrated whole. The aim of the Principle of Nationalism is to liberate the Chinese nation from foreign invasion and oppression and make it permanently free and independent, to attain full equality of all races within the country, and to render assistance to all weak races in the world with a view to realizing complete equality in the whole world.

The aim of the Principle of Democracy is to do away with political inequalities so that the nation belongs to every citizen. To carry out this Principle, the people enjoy the four political rights, i.e., election, recall, initiative and referendum. The Government has five powers, i.e., executive, legislative, judicial, examination and control. Such division of *rights* and *powers* is an ideal and progressive system under democracy.

The aim of the Principle of People's Livelihood is to help people solve the economic problems so that all persons may attain economic equality and enjoy a life of freedom and happiness. The methods for realizing this Principle are: (1) equalization of land ownership, and (2) control of private capital.

DR. HU SHIH ON THE CHINESE RENAISSANCE, 1933[9]

Dr. Hu Shih (1891-) is one of the great figures of modern Chinese intellectual history. While studying in America he took the lead in proposing the use of the colloquial language of China, the pai hua, *as the medium for the future literature of the New China. This reading is from a series of lectures given at the University of Chicago in 1933, in which Dr. Hu described some of the chief cultural and intellectual changes of the previous twenty years in China.*

✓ ✓ ✓

"The Renaissance" was the name given by a group of Peking University Students to a new monthly magazine which they published in 1918. They were mature students well trained in the old cultural tradition of the country, and they readily recognized in the new movement then led by some of their professors a striking similarity to the Renaissance in Europe. Three prominent features in the movement reminded them of the European Renaissance. First, it was a conscious movement to promote a new literature in the living language of the people to take the place of the classical literature of old. Second, it was a movement of conscious protest against many of the ideas and institutions in the traditional culture, and of conscious emancipation of the individual man and woman from the bondage of the forces of tradition. It was a movement of reason versus tradition, freedom versus authority, and glorification of life and human

---

[9] Hu Shih, *The Chinese Renaissance* (Chicago, 1934), pp. 44-47. Copyright, Haskell Lecture Foundation. Published, University of Chicago Press, 1934. Reprinted by permission of the publisher.

values versus their suppression. And lastly, strange enough, this new movement was led by men who knew their cultural heritage and tried to study it with the new methodology of modern historical criticism and research. In that sense it was also a humanist movement. In all these directions the new movement which began in 1917 and which was sometimes called the "New Culture Movement," the "New Thought" movement or "The New Tide" was capturing the imagination and sympathy of the youth of the nation as something which promised and pointed to the new birth of an old people and an old civilization.

Historically, there had been many periods of Chinese Renaissance. The rise of the great poets in the T'ang Dynasty, the simultaneous movement for a new prose literature modeled after the style of the Classical period, and the development of Zen Buddhism as a Chinese reformation of that Indian religion—these represented the First Chinese Renaissance. The great reform movements in the eleventh century, the subsequent development of a powerful secular neo-Confucianist philosophy which gradually overshadowed and finally replaced the medieval religions—all these important developments of the Sung Dynasty may be regarded as the Second Renaissance. The rise of the dramas in the thirteenth century, and the rise of the great novels in a later period, together with their frank glorification of love and the joys of life, may be called the Third Renaissance. And lastly, the revolt in the seventeenth century against the rational philosophy of the Sung and Ming dynasties, and the development of a new technique in classical scholarship in the last three hundred years with its philological and historical approach and its strict emphasis on the importance of documentary evidence—these, too, may be called the Fourth Renaissance.

Each of these historical movements had its important rôle to play and contributed to the periodic renewals of vitality in an old civilization. But all these great movements which rightly deserve the term of "renaissances," suffered from one common defect, namely, the absence of a conscious recognition of their historical mission. There was no conscious effort nor articulate interpretation: all of them were natural developments of historical

tendencies and were easily overpowered or swept away by
the conservative force of tradition against which they had
only dimly and unconsciously combated. Without this
conscious element, the new movements remained natural
processes of revolution, and never achieved the work of
revolutions; they brought in new patterns, but never completely dethroned the old, which continued to co-exist
with them and in time absorbed them. The Zen movement, for instance, practically replaced all the other
schools of Buddhism; and yet, when Zen became the officially recognized orthodoxy, it lost its revolutionary
character and resumed all the features against which its
founders had explicitly revolted. The secular philosophy
of neo-Confucianism was to replace the medieval religions, but it soon made itself a new religion embodying
unwittingly many of the features of medievalism. The
new critical scholarship of the last three centuries began
as a revolt against, and ended as a refuge for, the fruitless
philosophizing and the sterile literary education, both
of which continued to dominate and enslave the vast
majority of the literati. The new dramas and the new
novels came and went, but the Government continued to
hold the literary examinations on the classics, and the
men of letters continued to write their poetry and prose
in the classical language.

The Renaissance movement of the last two decades
differs from all the early movements in being a fully
conscious and studied movement. Its leaders know what
they want, and they know what they must destroy in
order to achieve what they want. They want a new
language, a new literature, a new outlook on life and
society, and a new scholarship. They want a new language, not only as an effective instrumentality for popular education, but also as the effective medium for the
development of the literature of a new China. They want
a literature that shall be written in the living tongue of
a living people and shall be capable of expressing the
real feelings, thoughts, inspirations, and aspirations of a
growing nation. They want to instil into the people a new
outlook on life which shall free them from the shackles
of tradition and make them feel at home in the new
world and its new civilization. They want a new scholarship which shall not only enable us to understand intelli-

gently the cultural heritage of the past, but also prepare us for active participation in the work of research in the modern sciences. This, as I understand it, is the mission of the Chinese Renaissance.

The conscious element in this movement is the result of long contact with the people and civilization of the West. It is only through contact and comparison that the relative value or worthlessness of the various cultural elements can be clearly and critically seen and understood. What is sacred among one people may be ridiculous in another; and what is despised or rejected by one cultural group, may in a different environment become the cornerstone for a great edifice of strange grandeur and beauty. For ten long centuries, by a peculiar perversion of aesthetic appreciation, the bound feet of Chinese women were regarded as beautiful; but it took only a few decades of contact with foreign people and ideas to make the Chinese people see the ugliness and inhumanity of this institution. On the other hand, the novels which were read by the millions of Chinese but which were always despised by the Chinese literati, have in recent decades been elevated to the position of respectable literature, chiefly through the influence of the European literature. Contact with strange civilizations brings new standards of value with which the native culture is re-examined and re-evaluated, and conscious reformation and regeneration are the natural outcome of such transvaluation of values. Without the benefit of an intimate contact with the civilization of the West, there could not be the Chinese Renaissance.

— Reading No. 10 —

THE STIMSON DOCTRINE OF NONRECOGNITION, JANUARY 7, 1932 [10]

Since none of the eight other signatories besides Japan to the Nine-Power Treaty of 1922 (see Reading No. 7) were willing to use force to prevent Japanese aggression against China in 1931-1932, they were reduced at least for the time being to the use of diplomatic protests and to legal reservations of their violated rights in respect to China. The position of nonrecognition of Japan's illegal acts in China, announced by Secretary of State Stimson in 1932, was maintained steadily by the United States thereafter. We refused to recognize the so-called "Manchukuo" regime set up in Manchuria by the Japanese. Our growing opposition to Japan's further aggressions in the Far East finally led to Pearl Harbor.

✓   ✓   ✓

IDENTIC NOTE SENT BY THE AMERICAN GOVERNMENT
TO THE GOVERNMENTS OF CHINA AND JAPAN

January 7, 1932

With the recent military operations about Chinchow, the last remaining administrative authority of the Government of the Chinese Republic in South Manchuria, as it existed prior to September 18, 1931, has been destroyed. The American Government continues confident that the work of the neutral commission recently authorized by the Council of the League of Nations will facilitate an ultimate solution of the difficulties now existing between China and Japan. But in view of the present situation and of its own rights and obligations therein, the

---

[10] *Conditions in Manchuria*, pp. 53-54 (Senate Document No. 55, 72nd Cong., 1st Sess., Washington, 1932.)

American Government deems it to be its duty to notify both the Government of the Chinese Republic and the Imperial Japanese Government that it can not admit the legality of any situation de facto nor does it intend to recognize any treaty or agreement entered into between those governments, or agents thereof, which may impair the treaty rights of the United States or its citizens in China, including those which relate to the sovereignty, the independence, or the territorial and administrative integrity of the Republic of China, or to the international policy relative to China, commonly known as the open-door policy; and that it does not intend to recognize any situation, treaty, or agreement which may be brought about by means contrary to the covenants and obligations of the pact of Paris of August 27, 1928, to which treaty both China and Japan, as well as the United States, are parties.

— Reading No. 11 —

CHIANG KAI-SHEK'S STRATEGY FOR DEFENSE AGAINST JAPAN, 1934 [11]

After Japan's conquest of Manchuria in 1931-1932, it became clear that she would stop at nothing to gain control of all China. Chiefly responsible for the defense of the country, Generalissimo Chiang realized China's weakness and attempted to delay all-out war as long as possible. In 1934 he gave a series of secret talks to his officers, from which these excerpts are taken. He frankly

[11] Chiang Kai-shek, *Resisting External Aggression and Regenerating the Chinese Nation* (Hankow, n.d.), 12-13, 53.

*stated his realistic understanding of China's position, and
prophesied with remarkable clarity the eventual defeat
of Japan at the hands of the world powers. In this we
may possibly find clues to his current thinking about the
defense of freedom in China against the threat of world
Communism.*

✓   ✓   ✓

. . . How can we resist the enemy? . . . From the
standpoint of military preparedness, we do not possess
attributes which would enable us to preserve our position
as an independent nation. We are not fit to be called a
modern state. It goes without saying that we are unable
to put up a successful resistance to Japan and that we
have to stand the pressure of the enemy and his insult.
But we all must know that the problem before us does
not concern China alone, but it is the problem of all Asia.
In fact it is the Pacific problem.

The Japanese have been doing their best to obtain
domination of the Pacific Ocean. It is not so much the
problem between China and Japan, as it is the problem
between Japan and the whole world. Why? Our late
Party leader, Dr. Sun, plainly told us: "China occupies
the status of a semi-colony." What is a semi-colony? It
is a country which is oppressed or protected by a group
of nations, thus becoming a common colony to them all.
Its position is more painful than that of an ordinary
colony. China has found herself in that position.

Japan, however, has been trying to make China her
colony, and in order to attain this object, she will be
obliged to fight the world powers. If Japan cannot wage a
decisive war with the world powers, she will not be
able to dominate Asia, nor will she be able to solve the
Pacific problem. In that case, she cannot become the
mistress of Asia, and she cannot swallow China.

At the same time we must know that while our domestic situation is complicated, the international situation
is even more complex. Because of the fact that China is
virtually a semi-colony, Japan wishes to swallow her
alone. First of all, she must conquer the world. As long
as Japan is unable to conquer the world, she cannot destroy China or dominate Asia.

At present, the Japanese have made the necessary military preparations and are capable of invading China, and of fighting simultaneously one single country in the world, but she does not possess enough strength to conquer the world, or to bring the world under her domination. Under such circumstances our military men must pay special attention to the changes in the international situation as well as those in the domestic situation. We must carefully consider whether we have means at our disposal and good opportunities for offering resistance to Japan's aggression in order to regenerate our nation. . . .

Internationally and diplomatically, we stand for justice and righteousness, whereas Japan represents suspicion and enmity. If we could strengthen ourselves, we would find friends all over the world. No matter how powerful Japan is militarily, she is already placed in isolation. She has become the common object of hatred for the world. With the attainment of complete unity, in the case of a world war breaking out, it might not be necessary for us to face our enemy on the battlefield as victory diplomatically and strategically would already have been ours.

— Reading No. 12 —

THE "GREATER EAST ASIA CO-PROSPERITY SPHERE," 1940[12]

As their war with China broadened into an attack on the colonial possessions of West European powers in Southeast Asia, the Japanese announced this plan for the control of all of East Asia. For this entire region

[12] Radio Address delivered by Foreign Minister of Japan, Arita, June 29, 1940, in *Foreign Relations: Japan: 1931-1941* (Washington, 1943), Vol. II, pp. 93-94.

Japan was to constitute the "stabilizing force," and the peoples of this vast area were to coördinate their economic development with that of Japan. This would have meant merely a widespread, thoroughgoing colonialism. It would require the eviction of all Western power and influence, and the destruction of all independent regimes in Far Eastern countries. The chief Asian power which stood in the way of these plans was the National Government of China.

✓   ✓   ✓

. . . It seems to be a most natural step that peoples who are closely related with each other geographically, racially, culturally, and economically should first form a sphere of their own for co-existence and co-prosperity and establish peace and order within that sphere, and at the same time secure a relationship of common existence and prosperity with other spheres. The cause of strife which mankind has hitherto experienced lies generally in the failure to give due consideration to the necessity of some such natural and constructive world order and to remedy old irrationalities and injustices. . . . It is in this spirit that Japan is now engaged in the task of establishing a new order in East Asia. It is extremely regrettable, therefore, that there should be those who not only fail to understand Japan's great undertaking based upon this fundamental principle, but on the contrary, obstruct establishment of peace in East Asia by supporting regime of Chiang Kai-shek. We have urged them to reconsider such an attitude in past, and now we intend further to urge their serious reflection. We are determined to leave no stone unturned in order to eradicate all activities for assisting Chiang Kai-shek. Sometimes there are those who would disapprove a change in the *status quo* by force of arms regardless of the reasons therefor. It is for the purpose of bringing about a just and permanent peace that Japan has been fighting in China for the past 3 years. Her employment of armed force is an act looking beyond the immediate present. The sword she has drawn is intended to be nothing other than a life-giving sword that destroys evil and makes justice manifest. Countries of East Asia and regions of the South Seas are geographically, historically, racially, and economically very closely related to each other. They are destined to help each other and minister to one another's needs for their common well-being and prosperity, and to promote peace and progress in their regions. Uniting of all these regions under a single sphere on the basis of common existence and insuring thereby the stability of that sphere is, I think, a natural conclusion. The idea to establish first a righteous peace in each of the various regions and then establish collectively a just peace for the whole world has long existed also in Europe and America. This system presupposes the existence of a stabilizing force in each region, with which as a center the peoples within that region are to secure their co-existence and co-prosperity and as well the stability of their sphere. It also presupposes that these groups will respect [one] another's individual characteristics, political, cultural, and economic, and they will cooperate and fulfill one another's needs for their common good. . . . Japan, while carrying on vigorously her task of constructing a new order in East Asia, is paying serious attention to developments in the European war and to its repercussions in the various quarters of East Asia, including the South Seas region. I desire to declare that the destiny of these regions in any development therein, and any disposal thereof, is a matter for grave concern to Japan in view of her mission and responsibility as the stabilizing force in East Asia.

— Reading No. 13 —

U.S. FOREIGN SERVICE OFFICERS ON CHINA POLICY, 1944, 1945 [13]

The following are portions extracted from memoranda submitted to the Department of State toward the end of the war, by some of its career officers serving in China. The following attitudes are clearly embodied here: (1) hostility toward the Nationalists; (2) approval for the Chinese Communists; (3) belief in the Titoist potentialities of the Chinese Communists and in the policy of arming them to fight against Japan; (4) advocacy of a Nationalist-Communist coalition government in China; but (5) belief in the inevitability of a final and complete Communist victory in China, and advocacy of United States backing for a victorious Communist regime.

✓   ✓   ✓

[Extract from a Report by John P. Davies, Nov. 7, 1944]

Only if he is able to enlist foreign intervention on a scale equal to the Japanese invasion of China will Chiang probably be able to crush the Communists. But foreign intervention on such a scale would seem to be unlikely. Relying upon his dispirited shambling legions, his decadent corrupt bureaucracy, his sterile political moralisms and such nervous foreign support as he can muster, the Generalissimo may nevertheless plunge China into civil war. He cannot succeed, however, where the Japanese in more than seven years of determined striving have failed. The Communists are already too strong for him.

[13] *United States Relations with China with Special Reference to the Period 1944-1949* (Released August 1949, Division of Publication, Office of Public Affairs, Dept. of State), pp. 573, 574, 576.

If the Generalissimo neither precipitates a civil war nor reaches an understanding with the Communists, he is still confronted with defeat. Chiang's feudal China can not long coexist alongside a modern dynamic popular government in North China.

The Communists are in China to stay. And China's destiny is not Chiang's but theirs.

[Extract from a Report by John P. Davies, Nov. 15, 1944]

We should not now abandon Chiang Kai-shek. To do so at this juncture would be to lose more than we could gain. We must for the time being continue recognition of Chiang's government.

But we must be realistic. We must not indefinitely underwrite a politically bankrupt regime. And, if the Russians are going to enter the Pacific War, we must make a determined effort to capture politically the Chinese Communists rather than allow them to go by default wholly to the Russians. Furthermore, we must fully understand that by reason of our recognition of the Chiang Kai-shek Government as now constituted we are committed to a steadily decaying regime and severely restricted in working out military and political cooperation with the Chinese Communists.

A coalition Chinese Government in which the Communists find a satisfactory place is the solution of this impasse most desirable to us. It provides our greatest assurance of a strong united, democratic, independent and friendly China—our basic strategic aim in Asia and the Pacific. If Chiang and the Communists reach a mutually satisfactory agreement, there will have been achieved from our point of view the most desirable possible solution. If Chiang and the Communists are irreconcilable, then we shall have to decide which faction we are going to support.

In seeking to determine which faction we should support we must keep in mind these basic considerations: Power in China is on the verge of shifting from Chiang to the Communists.

If the Russians enter North China and Manchuria, we obviously cannot hope to win the Communists entirely over to us, but we can through the control of supplies and post-war aid expect to exert considerable influence in the direction of Chinese nationalism and independence from Soviet control.

[Extract from a Report by Raymond P. Ludden and John S. Service, Feb. 14, 1945]

At present there exists in China a situation closely paralleling that which existed in Yugoslavia prior to Prime Minister Churchill's declaration of support for Marshal Tito. That statement was as follows:

"The sanest and safest course for us to follow is to judge all parties and factions dispassionately by the test of their readiness to fight the Germans and thus lighten the burden of Allied troops. This is not a time for ideological preferences for one side or the other."

A similar public statement issued by the Commander in Chief with regard to China would not mean the withdrawal of recognition or the cessation of military aid to the Central Government; that would be both unnecessary and unwise. It would serve notice, however, of our preparation to make use of all available means to achieve our primary objective. It would supply for all Chinese a firm rallying point which has thus far been lacking. The internal effect in China would be so profound that the Generalissimo would be forced to make concessions of power and permit united-front coalition. The present opposition groups, no longer under the prime necessity of safeguarding themselves, would be won wholeheartedly to our side and we would have in China, for the first time, a united ally.

GENERAL MARSHALL REPORTS ON HIS MISSION TO CHINA, 1947[14]

General George C. Marshall's ill-fated mission to China following World War II was an attempt to stop the Communist-Nationalist civil war and unify China under a coalition government as a prerequisite to our further aid in the peaceful development of China. In spite of many official views in Washington to the contrary, neither Communists nor Nationalists could enter any government unless assured of effective control of power therein. General Marshall's attempt to treat these two opponents in a civil war as though they could be parties in a system of parliamentary government was thus doomed from the start. His report, indeed, is a running commentary on what he himself came to describe as "the weakness of civil government in China," at that time.

✓ ✓ ✓

The President has recently given a summary of the developments in China during the past year and the position of the American Government toward China. Circumstances now dictate that I should supplement this with impressions gained at first hand.

In this intricate and confused situation, I shall merely endeavor here to touch on some of the more important considerations—as they appeared to me—during my connection with the negotiations to bring about peace in

[14] *United States Relations with China with Special Reference to the Period 1944-1949* (Released August 1949, Division of Publication, Office of Public Affairs, Dept. of State), pp. 686-689.

China and a stable democratic form of government.

In the first place, the greatest obstacle to peace has been the complete, almost overwhelming suspicion with which the Chinese Communist Party and the Kuomintang regard each other.

On the one hand, the leaders of the Government are strongly opposed to a communistic form of government. On the other, the Communists frankly state that they are Marxists and intend to work toward establishing a communistic form of government in China, though first advancing through the medium of a democratic form of government of the American or British type.

The leaders of the Government are convinced in their minds that the Communist-expressed desire to participate in a government of the type endorsed by the Political Consultative Conference last January had for its purpose only a destructive intention. The Communists felt, I believe, that the government was insincere in its apparent acceptance of the PCC resolutions for the formation of the new government and intended by coercion of military force and the action of secret police to obliterate the Communist Party. Combined with this mutual deep distrust was the conspicuous error by both parties of ignoring the effect of the fears and suspicions of the other party in estimating the reason for proposals or opposition regarding the settlement of various matters under negotiation. They each sought only to take counsel of their own fears. They both, therefore, to that extent took a rather lopsided view of each situation and were susceptible to every evil suggestion or possibility. This complication was exaggerated to an explosive degree by the confused reports of fighting on the distant and tremendous fronts of hostile military contact. Patrol clashes were deliberately magnified into large offensive actions. The distortion of the facts was utilized by both sides to heap condemnation on the other. It was only through the reports of American officers in the field teams from Executive Headquarters that I could get even a partial idea of what was actually happening and the incidents were too numerous and the distances too great for the American personnel to cover all of the ground. I must comment here on the superb courage of the officers of our Army and Marines in struggling against almost insurmountable and maddening obstacles to bring some measure of peace to China.

I think the most important factors involved in the recent breakdown of negotiations are these: On the side of the National Government, which is in effect the Kuomintang, there is a dominant group of reactionaries who have been opposed, in my opinion, to almost every effort I have made to influence the formation of a genuine coalition government. This has usually been under the cover of political or party action, but since the Party was the Government, this action, though subtle or indirect, has been devastating in its effect. They were quite frank in publicly stating their belief that cooperation by the Chinese Communist Party in the government was inconceivable and that only a policy of force could definitely settle the issue. This group includes military as well as political leaders.

On the side of the Chinese Communist Party there are, I believe, liberals as well as radicals, though this view is vigorously opposed by many who believe that the Chinese Communist Party discipline is too rigidly enforced to admit of such differences of viewpoint. Nevertheless, it has appeared to me that there is a definite liberal group among the Communists, especially of young men who have turned to the Communists in disgust at the corruption evident in the local governments—men who would put the interest of the Chinese people above ruthless measures to establish a Communist ideology in the immediate future. The dyed-in-the-wool Communists do not hesitate at the most drastic measures to gain their end as, for instance, the destruction of communications in order to wreck the economy of China and produce a situation that would facilitate the overthrow or collapse of the Government, without any regard to the immediate suffering of the people involved. They completely distrust the leaders of the Kuomintang and appear convinced that every Government proposal is designed to crush the Chinese Communist Party. I must say that the quite evidently inspired mob actions of last February and March, some within a few blocks of where I was then engaged in completing negotiations, gave the Communists good excuse for such suspicions.

However, a very harmful and immensely provocative

phase of the Chinese Communist Party procedure has been in the character of its propaganda. I wish to state to the American people that in the deliberate misrepresentation and abuse of the action, policies and purposes of our Government this propaganda has been without regard for the truth, without any regard whatsoever for the facts, and has given plain evidence of a determined purpose to mislead the Chinese people and the world and to arouse a bitter hatred of Americans. It has been difficult to remain silent in the midst of such public abuse and wholesale disregard of facts, but a denial would merely lead to the necessity of daily denials; an intolerable course of action for an American official. In the interest of fairness, I must state that the Nationalist Government publicity agency has made numerous misrepresentations, though not of the vicious nature of the Communist propaganda. Incidentally, the Communist statements regarding the Anping incident which resulted in the death of three Marines and wounding of twelve others were almost pure fabrication, deliberately representing a carefully arranged ambuscade of a Marine convoy with supplies for the maintenance of Executive Headquarters and some UNRRA supplies, as a defence against a Marine assault. The investigation of this incident was a tortuous procedure of delays and maneuvers to disguise the true and privately admitted facts of the case.

Sincere efforts to achieve settlement have been frustrated time and again by extremist elements of both sides. The agreements reached by the Political Consultative Conference a year ago were a liberal and forward-looking charter which then offered China a basis for peace and reconstruction. However, irreconcilable groups within the Kuomintang, interested in the preservation of their own feudal control of China, evidently had no real intention of implementing them. Though I speak as a soldier, I must here also deplore the dominating influence of the military. Their dominance accentuates the weakness of civil government in China. At the same time, in pondering the situation in China, one must have clearly in mind not the workings of small Communist groups or committees to which we are accustomed in America, but rather of millions of people and an army of more than a million men.

I have never been in a position to be certain of the development of attitudes in the innermost Chinese Communist circles. Most certainly, the course which the Chinese Communist Party has pursued in recent months indicated an unwillingness to make a fair compromise. It has been impossible even to get them to sit down at a conference table with Government representatives to discuss given issues. Now the Communists have broken off negotiations by their last offer which demanded the dissolution of the National Assembly and a return to the military positions of January 13th which the Government could not be expected to accept.

Between this dominant reactionary group in the Government and the irreconcilable Communists who, I must state, did not so appear last February, lies the problem of how peace and well-being are to be brought to the long-suffering and presently inarticulate mass of the people of China. The reactionaries in the Government have evidently counted on substantial American support regardless of their actions. The Communists by their unwillingness to compromise in the national interest are evidently counting on an economic collapse to bring about the fall of the Government, accelerated by extensive guerrilla action against the long lines of rail communications—regardless of the cost in suffering to the Chinese people.

The salvation of the situation, as I see it, would be the assumption of leadership by the liberals in the Government and in the minority parties, a splendid group of men, but who as yet lack the political power to exercise a controlling influence. Successful action on their part under the leadership of Generalissimo Chiang Kai-shek would, I believe, lead to unity through good government.

In fact, the National Assembly has adopted a democratic constitution which in all major respects is in accordance with the principles laid down by the all-party Political Consultative Conference of last January. It is unfortunate that the Communists did not see fit to participate in the Assembly since the constitution that has been adopted seems to include every major point that they wanted.

Soon the Government in China will undergo major reorganization pending the coming into force of the constitution following elections to be completed before Christmas Day 1947. Now that the form for a democratic China has been laid down by the newly adopted constitution, practical measures will be the test. It remains to be seen to what extent the Government will give substance to the form by a genuine welcome of all groups actively to share in the responsibility of government.

The first step will be the reorganization of the State Council and the executive branch of Government to carry on administration pending the enforcement of the constitution. The manner in which this is done and the amount of representation accorded to liberals and to non-Kuomintang members will be significant. It is also to be hoped that during this interim period the door will remain open for Communists or other groups to participate if they see fit to assume their share of responsibility for the future of China.

It has been stated officially and categorically that the period of political tutelage under the Kuomintang is at an end. If the termination of one-party rule is to be a reality, the Kuomintang should cease to receive financial support from the Government.

I have spoken very frankly because in no other way can I hope to bring the people of the United States to even a partial understanding of this complex problem. I have expressed all these views privately in the course of negotiations; they are well known, I think, to most of the individuals concerned. I express them now publicly, as it is my duty, to present my estimate of the situation and its possibilities to the American people who have a deep interest in the development of conditions in the Far East promising an enduring peace in the Pacific.

— Reading No. 15 —

MAO TSE-TUNG ON WORLD COMMUNIST REVOLUTION, 1940[15]

Even before Pearl Harbor forcefully projected the United States into an unprecedented involvement in the affairs of East Asian peoples, Mao Tse-tung had already described his own party's image of the revolution in modern China. According to him, the Chinese revolution was "bound to become a part of the proletarian Socialist world revolution," with the help of the Soviet Union. In this brief statement he outlined clearly the stages of revolutionary development through which this would take place.

↗   ↗   ↗

From the above, it is clear for us to see that there are different categories of revolution. One is a world revolution of the bourgeois and capitalist category, which ceased to prevail after the outbreak of the first imperialist World War, or more precisely, after the Russian Revolution of 1917. Since then, a world revolution of another category was born. It is the proletarian Socialist world revolution, in which the proletariat of the capitalist countries is the main force; and the oppressed nations in the colonies and semicolonies—their ally. Those classes, parties, or individuals of the oppressed nations engaging in the revolution, notwithstanding what kind of classes, parties, or individuals they are, or whether or not they are subjectively conscious of the fact, inasmuch as they stand against imperialism—their revolution is bound to

[15] Mao Tse-tung, *China's New Democracy,* in *The Strategy and Tactics of World Communism,* Supplement III, *Communism in China* (Washington, House Committee on Foreign Affairs, 1948), p. 72.

become a part of the proletarian Socialist world revolution, and they themselves are bound to become allies of the proletarian Socialist world revolution.

But the Chinese revolution assumes even more significance today when World War II is being waged in the fiercest manner, when the Soviet Union is passing from socialism to communism, and has emerged as a force capable of leading and helping the proletariat, the oppressed nations and revolutionary peoples all over the world in their struggle against imperialism and capitalist reaction; when the proletariat of the capitalist countries is preparing to overthrow capitalism and to build up socialism; and when today, under the leadership of the Communist Party of China, the Chinese proletariat, peasantry, intelligentsia, and the petty bourgeoisie have united and formed a strong and independent political force, then under such circumstances, is it not proper to attach the highest importance to the Chinese revolution in estimating its world significance? I should say, yes. The Chinese revolution is indeed a glorious and important part of the world revolution.

Such is the analysis of the first stage of the Chinese revolution (it may still be divided into several minor stages), the social nature of which makes it a bourgeois-democratic revolution of the new type. Although it is no proletarian socialist revolution of the newest type, certainly it has already formed a part, an important part of it and has been a great ally of it. The first step, i.e., the first stage of the revolution does not, and cannot at all build up a capitalist society under the dictatorship of the Chinese bourgeoisie. Its aim, in the very course of this first stage, is the setting up of a new democratic society of the united dictatorship of all revolutionary classes. The first stage thus accomplished, the development of the Chinese revolution will be carried forward into the second stage, viz, the building up of Chinese socialist society.

This then is the most fundamental peculiarity of the present phase of the Chinese revolution. Such is a brief description of the path traversed by the new revolution in the past 20 years (1919-40), since the May 4 student movement. This is the living and concrete content of the Chinese revolution of today.

— Reading No. 16 —

"ON PEOPLE'S DEMOCRATIC DICTATORSHIP," 1949[16]

Writing to commemorate the 28th anniversary of the Communist Party of China, July 1, 1949, Mao Tse-tung candidly described the main features of government in Communist China. He stated its purpose as being "the elimination of classes, state power and parties." The main instruments of government for this purpose were, however, to be the Communist party, the "people's state apparatus," and the revolutionary, i.e., nonreactionary, classes, all of which must therefore persist and grow stronger. The government of Communist China, operating by and through these instruments, was to be dictatorial, strong and nonbenevolent.

✓   ✓   ✓

"You are dictatorial." My dear sirs, what you say is correct. That is just what we are. All the experiences of the Chinese people, accumulated in the course of successive decades, tell us to carry out a people's democratic dictatorship.

This means that the reactionaries must be deprived of the right to voice their opinions; only the people have that right.

Who are the "people"? At the present stage in China, they are the working class, the peasantry, the petty bourgeoisie and the national bourgeoisie.

Under the leadership of the working class and the Communist Party, these classes unite to create their own state and elect their own government so as to enforce their dictatorship over the henchmen of imperialism—

[16] Mao Tse-tung, *On People's Democratic Dictatorship* (Peking, 1950), pp. 15-19.

the landlord class and bureaucratic capitalist class, as well as the reactionary clique of the Kuomintang, which represents these classes, and their accomplices. The people's government will suppress such persons. It will only permit them to behave themselves properly. It will not allow them to speak or act wildly. Should they do so, they will be instantly curbed and punished. The democratic system is to be carried out within the ranks of the people, giving them freedom of speech, assembly and association. The right to vote is given only to the people, not to the reactionaries.

These two things, democracy for the people and dictatorship for the reactionaries, when combined, constitute the people's democratic dictatorship.

Why must things be done in this way? Everyone is very clear on this point. If things were not done like this, the revolution would fail, the people would suffer and the state would perish.

"Don't you want to abolish state power?" Yes, we want to, but not at the present time. We cannot afford to abolish state power just now. Why not? Because imperialism still exists. Because, internally, reactionaries still exist and classes still exist.

Our present task is to strengthen the people's state apparatus—meaning principally the people's army, the people's police and the people's courts—thereby safeguarding national defence and protecting the people's interests. Given these conditions, China, under the leadership of the working class and the Communist Party, can develop steadily from an agricultural into an industrial country and from a New Democratic into a Socialist and, eventually, Communist society, eliminating classes and realizing universal harmony.

Such state apparatus as the army, the police and the courts are instruments with which one class oppresses another. As far as the hostile classes are concerned, these are instruments of oppression. They are violent and certainly not "benevolent" things.

"You are not benevolent." Exactly. We definitely have no benevolent policies toward the reactionaries or the counter-revolutionary activities of the reactionary classes. Our benevolent policy does not apply to such deeds or such persons, who are outside the ranks of the people; it applies only to the people.

The people's state is for the protection of the people. Once they have a people's state, the people then have the possibility of applying democratic methods on a nationwide and comprehensive scale to educate and reform themselves, so that they may get rid of the influences of domestic and foreign reactionaries. (These influences are still very strong at present and will remain for a long time to come; they cannot be eradicated quickly.) Thus the people can reform their bad habits and thoughts derived from the old society, so that they will not take the wrong road pointed out to them by the reactionaries, but will continue to advance and develop toward a Socialist and then Communist society.

The methods we use in this respect are democratic, that is, methods of persuasion and not of compulsion. If people break the law they will be punished, imprisoned or even sentenced to death. But these will be individual cases, differing in principle from the dictatorship imposed against the reactionaries as a class.

As for those belonging to reactionary classes or groups, after their political power has been overthrown, we will also give them land and work, permitting them to make a living and to reform themselves through labour into new persons—but only on condition that they do not rebel, sabotage or create disturbances. If they do not want to work, the people's state will force them to do so. Furthermore, the propaganda and educational work directed toward them will be carried out with the same care and thoroughness as the work already conducted among captured army officers. This may also be spoken of as a "benevolent policy," but it will be compulsorily imposed upon those originally from enemy classes. This can in no way be compared to our work along self-educational lines among the ranks of the revolutionary people.

This job of reforming the reactionary classes can be handled only by a state having a people's democratic dictatorship. When the work has been completed, China's major exploiting classes—the landlord class and the bureaucratic capitalist class, i.e., the monopoly capitalist class—will have been finally eliminated.

Then there will remain only the national bourgeoisie. In the present stage a great deal of suitable educational work can be done among them. When the time comes to realize Socialism, that is, to nationalise private enterprise, we will go a step further in our work of educating and reforming them. The people have a strong state apparatus in their hands, and they do not fear rebellion on the part of the national bourgeoisie.

The education of the peasantry presents a serious problem. Peasant economy is dispersed. According to the Soviet Union's experience, it takes a long time and much painstaking work before agriculture can be socialised. Without the socialisation of agriculture, there can be no complete and consolidated socialism.

If we wish to socialise agriculture, we must develop a strong industry having state-operated enterprises as its main component.

— Reading No. 17 —

ART, LITERATURE, AND POLITICS UNDER CHINESE COMMUNISM, 1942[17]

In May 1942, at Yenan, then the headquarters of the Chinese Communists, a conference was held on problems of art and literature. Mao Tse-tung made two addresses to this conference, from which these excerpts are taken. In strict Marxist-Leninist-Stalinist orthodoxy he stresses the relation between art and literature, on the one hand, and the Communist revolution, and in this relationship, the domination of politics in and over art and literature.

✔   ✔   ✔

[17] Mao Tse-tung, *Problems of Art and Literature* (Bombay, 1952), pp. 7-8, 28-29, 31-33.

Since literature and art are created for the workers, peasants, soldiers, and for the cadres among them, the problem arises of how to understand and get to know the people. In order to understand and know all sorts of things and to understand and become acquainted with all sorts of people, one must do extensive work among them wherever they are to be found—in Party and government organs, in villages and factories, in the Eighth Route and New Fourth Armies. Writers and artists should, of course, pursue their creative activities, but their first and foremost duty is to get to know the people and to understand their ways.

What have our writers and artists been doing in this respect? I do not think that they have learned to know or understand the people. Not knowing the people, they are like heroes without a battlefield. Writers and artists are not only unfamiliar with the subjects they describe and with their reading public, but, in some cases, are even completely estranged from them. Our writers and artists do not know the workers, peasants and soldiers, or the cadres emerging from among them. What do they not understand? The language. They speak the language of the intellectuals, not the language of the masses.

Let us consider the first problem. All culture or all present-day literature and art belong to a certain class, to a certain party or to a certain political line. There is no such thing as art for art's sake, or literature and art that lie above class distinctions or above partisan interests. There is no such thing as literature and art running parallel to politics or being independent of politics. They are in reality non-existent.

In a society with class and party distinctions, literature and art belong to a class or party, which means that they respond to the political demands of a class or party as well as to the revolutionary task of a given revolutionary period. When literature and art deviate from this principle, they divorce themselves from the basic needs of the people.

The literature and art of the proletariat are part of the revolutionary programme of the proletariat. As Lenin pointed out, they are "a screw in the machine." Thus the role of the Party's work in literature and art is determined by the overall revolutionary programme of the

Party. Deviation from this principle inevitably leads to dualism and pluralism and eventually to such views as Trotsky advocated: Marxist politics but bourgeois art.

We are not in favour of overemphasizing the importance of literature and art but neither must we underestimate them. Although literature and art are subordinate to politics, they in turn exert a tremendous influence upon politics. Revolutionary literature and art are part of a revolutionary programme. They are like the aforementioned screws. They may be of greater or lesser importance, of primary or secondary value when compared with other parts of the machine, but they are nevertheless indispensable to the machine; they are indispensable parts of the entire revolutionary movement. If we had no literature and art, even of the most general kind, we should not be able to carry on the revolution or to achieve victory. It would be a mistake not to recognise this fact.

Furthermore, when we say that literature and art are subordinate to politics we mean class politics and mass politics, not the so-called politics of a few politicians. Politics, whether revolutionary or counter-revolutionary, represent the struggle between two opposing classes, not the behaviour of isolated individuals. The war of an ideology and the war of literature and art, especially the war of a revolutionary ideology and the war of revolutionary literature and art, must be subordinate to the political war because the needs of a class and of the masses can be expressed in a concentrated form only through politics. . . .

There are two standards for literary and art criticism. One is the political standard and the other the artistic standard.

By the political standard, artistic production is good or comparatively good, if it serves the interests of our war of resistance and unity, if it encourages solidarity among the masses and if it opposes retrogression and promotes progress. Conversely, artistic production is bad or comparatively bad, if it encourages dissension and division among the masses, if it impedes progress and holds the people back. . . .

In examining the subjective intent of a writer, that is to say, in determining whether his motive is correct or good, we cannot depend upon his own declaration of intent; we must analyse the effect which his behaviour (his creative product) has on society and the masses. The standard for examining a subjective intent is social practice; and the standard for examining a motive is the effect it produces.

Our criticism of literature and art must not be sectarian. Bearing in mind the general principles of the war of resistance and national unity, we must tolerate all works of literature and art expressing every kind and shade of political attitude. At the same time, we must be firm in principle and in our position when we criticise. This means that we must criticise severely all literary and artistic works which present viewpoints that are opposed to national, scientific, mass and Communist interests because both the motives and the effects of this so-called literature and art jeopardise our war of resistance and wreck our national unity. . . .

We know now that there is a political standard and an artistic standard. What then is the proper relation between them? Politics is not at the same time art. The world outlook in general is not at the same time the methods of artistic creation. Not only do we reject abstract and rigid political standards but we also reject abstract and rigid artistic standards. Different class societies have different political and artistic standards as do the various classes within a given class society. But in any class society or in any class within that society, political standards come first and artistic standards come second.

— Reading No. 18 —

CHINESE COMMUNIST ATTITUDE TOWARD RELIGION, 1958[18]

Quoting Engels, Lenin, and Mao Tse-tung, the writer of this article points out the proper Communist position on religion. This position combines orthodox atheism for Communists with a policy of tolerating religion as long as religious persons and organizations agree to "travel the road of socialism [communism]." But, since people who become communists must also become atheists, progress toward "socialism" means by definition the eventual destruction of all religious belief. Thus Chinese Communists require that their religious believers today acquiesce in nothing less than the eventual destruction of their religions.

↗   ↗   ↗

The religious problem concerns the faith of the masses and forms and ideological problem. On the other hand, as a tool of the class struggle in class society religion constitutes a political problem. The religious problem itself, therefore, involves contradictions among the people and those between us and our enemy. The problems to be resolved in respect of religious activities involve two different kinds of contradictions.

We believe that religion is a natural product of the human society at a certain stage of its development and a manifestation of man's appeal to mythical forces for

---

[18] Chang Chih-yi, "Atheists and Theists Can Coöperate Politically and Travel The Road of Socialism," in *Philosophical Research* [*Chê Hsüeh Yen Chiu*], Issue I, Feb. 15, 1958 (in American Consulate General, Hongkong, *Current Background*, No. 510, June 15, 1958) pp. 12-13, 16-17. Minor changes have been made in this translation, by reference to the original Chinese text.

help in face of inexplicable and irresistible natural forces. Simple religious concepts have developed in primitive society, but it is only in class society that they take the shape of systematized religion and subsequently flourish through the utilization by the exploiting class. Religion, therefore, is a reflection of class contradiction in class society, and is a tool of the class struggle, chiefly one employed by the exploiting class to rule the exploited class. It is also revealed on the other hand that the exploited class utilizes religion as a banner under which the people are rallied together to resist the exploiting class. In class society, therefore, religious contradictions are chiefly those between the people and their enemy. However, as there are believers and disbelievers in the exploited and oppressed class and different faiths are also embraced, religious contradictions in the meantime manifest themselves as contradictions among the people. Religion owes its existence to not only social causes but also cognitive causes, and therefore involves not only the struggle between man and society but also that between man and nature. We understand that the cognitive cause of the growth of religion indicates man's lack of cognition and grasp of the laws of the development of society and nature. We can come to the conclusion that after the complete eradication of class society, i.e. the complete eradication of the social causes that give rise to religion, the class contradictions and those between the people and their enemy will no longer exist. But the calamities and threats to man posed by nature will continue for a long period of time, during which man cannot completely conquer nature, and the contradictions between the believers and disbelievers and between believers of different faiths among the working people—contradictions among the people—will continue for a very long period of time. The issue is by no means so simple as subjectively imagined by certain people, who believe that it can be readily resolved with the obliteration of class society.

Religion in the history of our country, as in that of any other country, has served a two-fold purpose: in the first place it is utilized by the reactionary ruling class as a tool to consolidate its rule, and, secondly, the oppressed class also utilizes it as a band to rally the masses to resist the reactionary rule (which, however, does not constitute a major factor and is not always effective). Because religion has been utilized by imperialism, the landlord class and the bureaucratic class, the religious problem also reflects the contradictions between the broad mass of people on the one hand and imperialism, the landlord class and the bureaucratic class on the other during the democratic revolution in our country—contradictions between the people and their enemy. . . .

Some people hold that the Communists, being atheists, cannot cooperate with the theists in the political sphere nor can they honestly adopt a policy favoring freedom of religious belief. Such an idea is erroneous. The Communists are atheists and also every inch materialists. They never conceal their understanding and views on any problem. They believe that religion, like other things (including the Communist Party and the state), has to run through the process of growth, development and extinction; it must eventually go on the path of extinction. They also believe that in class society religion by nature is opium poisonous to the people and has chiefly become a weapon of the exploiting class to dupe and oppress the toiling masses ever since mankind entered class society. For cognitive reasons they do not have religious faith. Bearing in mind the elevation of the political consciousness of the working people in the struggle against the exploiting class, the Communists do not take a laissez faire attitude towards religious influences among the people. The Communists, as Marxist-Leninists and historical materialists, believe that religion which owes its existence to social and cognitive causes is a subjective entity and the state must not employ administrative decrees to interfere with religious belief nor adopt simple rash measures to handle the religious issue. Religion, unlike a social system, is a form of ideology whose specialty is to reflect realities in a distorted manner. Man can apply revolutionary violence to overthrow a reactionary social system but the same means cannot be used to destroy the religious consciousness in the minds of the people. We therefore believe that the obliteration of religion is not contingent on the obliteration of classes alone but must wait until the tremendous development of man's power for the control of nature. By that time both the social and cognitive causes responsible for the existence of religion will have been liquidated, mankind emancipated from the enthraldom of social forces and natural forces, and religion will gradually die a natural death. The Communists therefore believe that the employment of administrative decrees to interfere with the religious belief of the masses and the adoption of simple rash measures to handle the religious issue in the hope of liquidating religion are futile.

Engels in his "Program of the Exiles of the Blonkist Society" scoffed at the Blonkist attempt to use a decree to "obliterate God". He said: "First, a flood of decrees can be issued, but how futile they are. Second, persecution is the best way to boost an unpopular belief." Such a method to prohibit religion practically means rendering a service to God, he continued. [Note: since Chinese does not employ capitalisation, the use of the capital G in God obviously originates in the translator.]

Lenin in his "The Workers' Political Party's Attitude towards Religion", apart from recounting the aforementioned basic viewpoint of Engels, said that he "could never confine the anti-religious struggle to abstract ideological propaganda and wind it up as such. The struggle should be coordinated with the concrete phase of the class movement that seeks to uproot the social causes of religion." The attempt to overthrow religion with atheist propaganda he denounced in the article as superficial bourgeois narrow culturalistic viewpoint. In capitalist countries, he said, the social causes of religion are "the dread of the blind influence of capital," and "only when the masses themselves have learned how to band themselves together and become well organized and consciously oppose such religious cause and all manifestations of capitalist rule can the religious concept be obliterated." ("Marx, Engels and Marxism," Chinese edition, pp. 233-234).

Chairman Mao said in his "New Democracy": "Members of the Communist Party can establish the anti-imperialist united front in the area of political action in cooperation with certain idealists and even believers of religion, but can never approve their idealism or religious belief." In his discourse on "Correct Handling of the Contradictions among the People" he gave a very clear comment on the problem: "The application of simple methods to deal with the ideological problem arising among the people or problems relative to the spiritual world is not only futile but very harmful. . . . We cannot employ administrative decrees to eliminate religion; we cannot force people not to believe, nor can we force them to abandon idealism. . . ."

These Marxist classical writers and communist revolutionary leaders do not conceal the basic ideological difference between the communists and the religious followers, but they do not object to political collaboration between the communists and religious followers. . . . The atheists (the Communists), while in a position to cooperate with the theists (religious circles) in the field of politics, must lead the latter in the same field. Moreover, only when the religious followers have accepted the leadership of the Chinese Communist Party can they be helped to acquire a clear understanding of the anti-imperialist direction, to discriminate right from wrong and to distinguish our enemy. Then they can travel the road of socialism in company with the people throughout the country.

— Reading No. 19 —

SINO-SOVIET TREATY OF FEBRUARY 14, 1950[19]

Very soon after taking power on the mainland, the Chinese Communists made a series of agreements with the Soviet Union. Included were a treaty of friendship and alliance, an agreement on railways and ports in Manchuria, and an agreement covering payment to the U.S.S.R. for equipment and other materials to be sup-

[19] *Soviet Russia Today*, April 1950, p. 25.

plied to Communist China. The text of the treaty of friendship and alliance follows.

✓   ✓   ✓

ARTICLE I. Both High Contracting Parties undertake jointly to take all the necessary measures at their disposal for the purpose of preventing a repetition of aggression and violation of peace on the part of Japan or any other state which should unite with Japan, directly or indirectly, in acts of aggression. In the event of one of the High Contracting Parties being attacked by Japan or states allied with it, and thus being involved in a state of war, the other High Contracting Party will immediately render military and other assistance with all the means at its disposal.

The High Contracting Parties also declare their readiness in the spirit of sincere cooperation to participate in all international actions aimed at insuring peace and security throughout the world, and will do all in their power to achieve the speediest implementation of these tasks.

ARTICLE II. Both the High Contracting Parties undertake by means of mutual agreement to strive for the earliest conclusion of a peace treaty with Japan, jointly with the other Powers which were allies during the Second World War.

ARTICLE III. Both High Contracting Parties undertake not to conclude any alliance directed against the other High Contracting Party, and not to take part in any coalition or in actions or measures directed against the other high Contracting Party.

ARTICLE IV. Both High Contracting Parties will consult each other in regard to all important international problems affecting the common interests of the Soviet Union and China, being guided by the interests of the consolidation of peace and universal security.

ARTICLE V. Both the High Contracting Parties undertake, in the spirit of friendship and cooperation and in conformity with the principles of equality, mutual interests, and also mutual respect for the state sovereignty and territorial integrity and non-interference in internal affairs of the other High Contracting Party—to develop and consolidate economic and cultural ties between the

Soviet Union and China, to render each other every possible economic assistance, and to carry out the necessary economic cooperation.

ARTICLE VI. The present Treaty comes into force immediately upon its ratification; the exchange of instruments of ratification will take place in Peking.

The present Treaty will be valid for 30 years. If neither of the High Contracting Parties gives notice one year before the expiration of this term of its desire to denounce the Treaty, it shall remain in force for another five years and will be extended in compliance with this rule.

Done in Moscow on February 14, 1950, in two copies, each in the Russian and Chinese languages, both texts having equal force.

— Reading No. 20 —

CONSTITUTION OF THE REPUBLIC OF CHINA, 1947[20]

This Constitution was adopted by a National Assembly called at Nanking in November 1946, attended by more than 2,000 representatives. These were largely of the Nationalist party (Kuomintang), as the Communists refused to participate. The National Assembly approved the document on December 25, 1946, and the National Government promulgated it on January 1, 1947, to become effective on December 25, 1947. It provided for a parliamentary system with a cabinet responsible to the legislature. But genuine parliamentary responsibility would take much time to develop, particularly under the mili-

[20] *China Yearbook, 1957-58* (Taipei, 1958), pp. 687-710.

tary emergency of the continuing civil war with the Communists. Excerpts from this Constitution are given here.

✓   ✓   ✓

CHAPTER II. RIGHTS AND DUTIES OF THE PEOPLE

ARTICLE 7. All citizens of the Republic of China, irrespective of sex, religion, race, class, or party affiliation, shall be equal before the law.

ARTICLE 8. Personal freedom shall be guaranteed to the people. Except in case of *flagrante delicto* as provided by law, no person shall be arrested or detained otherwise than by a judicial or a police organ in accordance with the procedure prescribed by law. No person shall be tried or punished otherwise than by a law court in accordance with the procedure prescribed by law. Any arrest, detention, trial, or punishment which is not in accordance with the procedure prescribed by law may be resisted.

When a person is arrested or detained on suspicion of having committed a crime, the organ making the arrest or detention shall in writing inform the said person and his designated relative or friend of the grounds for his arrest or detention, and shall, within twenty-four hours, turn him over to a competent court for trial. The said person, or any other person, may petition the competent court that a writ be served within twenty-four hours on the organ making the arrest for the surrender of the said person for trial.

The court shall not reject the petition mentioned in the preceding paragraph, nor shall it order the organ concerned to make an investigation and report first. The organ concerned shall not refuse to execute, or delay in executing, the writ of the court for the surrender of the said person for trial.

When a person is unlawfully arrested or detained by any organ, he or any other person may petition the court for an investigation. The court shall not reject such a petition, and shall, within twenty-four hours, investigate the action of the organ concerned and deal with the matter in accordance with law.

ARTICLE 9. Except those in active military service, no person shall be subject to trial by a military tribunal.

ARTICLE 10. The people shall have freedom of residence and of change of residence.

ARTICLE 11. The people shall have freedom of speech, teaching, writing, and publication.

ARTICLE 12. The people shall have freedom of privacy of correspondence.

ARTICLE 13. The people shall have freedom of religious belief.

ARTICLE 14. The people shall have freedom of assembly and of association.

ARTICLE 15. The right of existence, the right of work, and the right of property shall be guaranteed to the people.

ARTICLE 16. The people shall have the right of presenting petitions, lodging complaints, or instituting legal proceedings.

ARTICLE 17. The people shall have the rights of election, recall, initiative, and referendum.

ARTICLE 18. The people shall have the right of taking public examinations and of holding public offices.

ARTICLE 19. The people shall have the duty of paying taxes in accordance with law.

ARTICLE 20. The people shall have the duty of performing military service in accordance with law.

ARTICLE 21. The people shall have the right and the duty of receiving citizens' education.

ARTICLE 22. All other freedoms and rights of the people that are not detrimental to social order or public welfare shall be guaranteed under the Constitution.

ARTICLE 23. All the freedoms and rights enumerated in the preceding Articles shall not be restricted by law except by such as may be necessary to prevent infringement upon the freedoms of other persons, to avert an imminent crisis, to maintain social order, or to advance public welfare.

ARTICLE 24. Any public functionary who, in violation of law, infringes upon the freedom or right of any person shall, in addition to being subject to disciplinary measures in accordance with law, be held responsible under criminal and civil laws. The injured person may, in accordance with law, claim compensation from the State for damage sustained.

Chapter III. The National Assembly

ARTICLE 25. The National Assembly shall, in accordance with the provisions of this Constitution, exercise political powers on behalf of the whole body of citizens.

ARTICLE 26. The National Assembly shall be composed of the following Delegates:

(1) One Delegate shall be elected from each Hsien, Municipality, or area of equivalent status. In case its population exceeds 500,000, one additional Delegate shall be elected for each additional 500,-000. Areas equivalent to Hsien or Municipalities shall be prescribed by law.

(2) Delegates to represent Mongolia shall be elected on the basis of four for each League and one for each Special Banner.

(3) The number of Delegates to be elected from Tibet shall be prescribed by law.

(4) The number of Delegates to be elected by various racial groups in frontier regions shall be prescribed by law.

(5) The number of Delegates to be elected by Chinese citizens residing abroad shall be prescribed by law.

(6) The number of Delegates to be elected by occupational groups shall be prescribed by law.

(7) The number of Delegates to be elected by women's organizations shall be prescribed by law.

ARTICLE 27. The functions of the National Assembly shall be as follows:

(1) To elect the President and the Vice President;

(2) To recall the President or the Vice President;

(3) To amend the Constitution;

(4) To vote on proposed Constitutional amendments submitted by the Legislative Yuan by way of referendum.

With respect to the rights of initiative and referendum, except as is provided in Items (3) and (4) of the preceding paragraph, the National Assembly shall make regulations pertaining thereto and put them into effect, after the above-mentioned two political rights have been exercised in one half of the Hsien and Municipalities of the whole country.

ARTICLE 28. Delegates to the National Assembly shall be elected every six years.

The term of office of the Delegates to each National Assembly shall terminate on the day on which the next National Assembly convenes.

No incumbent Government official shall, in the electoral area where he holds office, be elected Delegate to the National Assembly.

ARTICLE 29. The National Assembly shall be convoked by the President to meet ninety days prior to the date of expiration of each presidential term.

ARTICLE 30. An extraordinary session of the National Assembly shall be convoked in any of the following circumstances:

(1) When, in accordance with the provisions of Article 49 of this Constitution, a new President and a new Vice President are to be elected;

(2) When, by resolution of the Control Yuan, an impeachment of the President or the Vice President is instituted;

(3) When, by resolution of the Legislative Yuan, an amendment to the Constitution is proposed;

(4) When a meeting is requested by not less than two-fifths of the Delegates to the National Assembly.

When an extraordinary session is to be convoked in accordance with Item (1) or Item (2) of the preceding paragraph, the President of the Legislative Yuan shall issue the notice of convocation; when it is to be convoked in accordance with Item (3) or Item (4), it shall be convoked by the President of the Republic.

ARTICLE 31. The National Assembly shall meet at the seat of the Central Government.

ARTICLE 32. No Delegate to the National Assembly shall be held responsible outside the Assembly for opinions expressed or votes cast at meetings of the Assembly.

ARTICLE 33. While the Assembly is in session, no Delegate to the National Assembly shall, except in case of *flagrante delicto*, be arrested or detained without the permission of the National Assembly.

ARTICLE 34. The organization of the National Assembly, the election and recall of Delegates to the National Assembly, and the procedure whereby the National Assembly is to carry out its functions shall be prescribed by law.

CHAPTER IV. THE PRESIDENT

ARTICLE 35. The President shall be the head of the State and shall represent the Republic of China in foreign relations.

ARTICLE 36. The President shall have supreme command of the land, sea, and air forces of the whole country.

ARTICLE 37. The President shall, in accordance with law, promulgate laws and issue mandates with the countersignature of the President of the Executive Yuan or with the countersignatures of both the President of the Executive Yuan and the Ministers or Chairmen of Commissions concerned.

ARTICLE 38. The President shall, in accordance with the provisions of this Constitution, exercise the powers of concluding treaties, declaring war, and making peace.

ARTICLE 39. The President may, in accordance with law, declare martial law with the approval of, or subject to confirmation by, the Legislative Yuan. When the Legislative Yuan deems it necessary, it may by resolution request the President to terminate martial law.

ARTICLE 40. The President shall, in accordance with law, exercise the power of granting amnesties, pardons, remission of sentences, and restitution of civil rights.

ARTICLE 41. The President shall, in accordance with law, appoint and remove civil and military officers.

ARTICLE 42. The President may, in accordance with law, confer honors and decorations.

ARTICLE 43. In case of a natural calamity, an epidemic, or a national financial or economic crisis that calls for emergency measures, the President, during the recess of the Legislative Yuan, may, by resolution of the Executive Yuan Council and in accordance with the Law on Emergency Orders, issue emergency orders, proclaiming such measures as may be necessary to cope with the situation. Such orders shall, within one month after issuance, be presented to the Legislative Yuan for confirmation; in case the Legislative Yuan withholds confirmation, the said orders shall forthwith cease to be valid.

ARTICLE 44. In case of dispute between two or more Yuan other than those concerning which there are relevant provisions in this Constitution, the President may call a meeting of the Presidents of the Yuan concerned for consultation with a view to reaching a solution.

ARTICLE 45. Any citizen of the Republic of China who has attained the age of forty years may be elected President or Vice President.

ARTICLE 46. The election of the President and the Vice President shall be prescribed by law.

ARTICLE 47. The President and the Vice President shall serve a term of six years. They may be re-elected for a second term.

ARTICLE 48. The President shall, at the time of assuming office, take the following oath:

> "I do solemnly and sincerely swear before the people of the whole country that I will observe the Constitution, faithfully perform my duties, promote the welfare of the people, and safeguard the security of the State, and will in no way betray the people's trust. Should I break my oath, I shall be willing to submit myself to severe punishment by the State. This is my solemn oath."

ARTICLE 49. In case the office of the President should become vacant, the Vice President shall succeed until the expiration of the original presidential term. In case the office of both the President and the Vice President should become vacant, the President of the Executive Yuan shall act for the President; and, in accordance with the provisions of Article 30 of this Constitution, an extraordinary session of the National Assembly shall be convoked for the election of a new President and a new Vice President, who shall hold office until the completion of the term left unfinished by the preceding President. In case the President should be unable to attend to office due to any cause, the Vice President shall act for the President. In case both the President and the Vice President should be unable to attend to office, the President of the Executive Yuan shall act for the President.

ARTICLE 50. The President shall be relieved of his functions on the day on which his term of office expires. If by that time the succeeding President has not yet been elected, or if the President-elect and the Vice President-elect have not yet assumed office, the President of the Executive Yuan shall act for the President.

ARTICLE 51. The period during which the President of the Executive Yuan may act for the President shall not exceed three months.

ARTICLE 52. The President shall not, without having been recalled, or having been relieved of his functions, be liable to criminal prosecution unless he is charged with having committed an act of rebellion or treason.

CHAPTER XIII. FUNDAMENTAL NATIONAL POLICIES

Section 3. National Economy

ARTICLE 142. National economy shall be based on the Principle of People's Livelihood and shall seek to effect equalization of land ownership and restriction of private capital in order to attain a well-balanced sufficiency in national wealth and people's livelihood.

ARTICLE 143. All land within the territory of the Republic of China shall belong to the whole body of citizens. Private ownership of land, acquired by the people in accordance with law, shall be protected and restricted by law. Privately owned land shall be liable to taxation according to its value, and the Government may buy such land according to its value.

Mineral deposits which are embedded in the land, and natural power which may, for economic purposes, be utilized for the public benefit shall belong to the State, regardless of the fact that private individuals may have acquired ownership over such land.

If the value of a piece of land has increased not through the exertion of labor or the employment of capital, the State shall levy thereon an increment tax, the proceeds of which shall be enjoyed by the people in common.

In the distribution and readjustment of land, the State shall, in principle, assist self-farming land-owners and persons who make use of the land by themselves, and shall also regulate their appropriate areas of operation.

ARTICLE 144. Public utilities and other enterprises of a

monopolistic nature shall, in principle, be under public operation. In cases permitted by law, they may be operated by private citizens.

ARTICLE 145. With respect to private wealth and privately owned enterprises, the State shall restrict them by law if they are deemed detrimental to a balanced development of national wealth and people's livelihood.

Coöperative enterprises shall receive encouragement and assistance from the State.

Private citizens' productive enterprises and foreign trade shall receive encouragement, guidance, and protection from the State.

ARTICLE 146. The State shall, by the use of scientific technique, develop water conservancy, increase the productivity of land, improve agricultural conditions, plan for the utilization of land, develop agricultural resources, and hasten the industrialization of agriculture.

ARTICLE 147. The Central Government, in order to attain a balanced economic development among the Provinces, shall give appropriate aid to poor or unproductive Provinces.

The Provinces, in order to attain a balanced economic development among the Hsien, shall give appropriate aid to poor or unproductive Hsien.

ARTICLE 148. Within the territory of the Republic of China, all goods shall be permitted to move freely from place to place.

ARTICLE 149. Financial institutions shall, in accordance with law, be subject to State control.

ARTICLE 150. The State shall extensively establish financial institutions for the common people, with a view to relieving unemployment.

ARTICLE 151. With respect to Chinese citizens residing abroad, the State shall foster and protect the development of their economic enterprises.

Section 4. Social Security

ARTICLE 152. The State shall provide suitable opportunity for work to people who are able to work.

ARTICLE 153. The State, in order to improve the livelihood of laborers and farmers and to improve their productive skill, shall enact laws and carry out policies for their protection.

Women and children engaged in labor shall, according to their age and physical condition, be accorded special protection.

ARTICLE 154. Capital and labor shall, in accordance with the principle of harmony and cooperation, promote productive enterprises. Conciliation and arbitration of disputes between capital and labor shall be prescribed by law.

ARTICLE 155. The State, in order to promote social welfare, shall establish a social insurance system. To the aged and the infirm who are unable to earn a living, and to victims of unusual calamities, the State shall give appropriate assistance and relief.

ARTICLE 156. The State, in order to consolidate the foundation of national existence and development, shall protect motherhood and carry out the policy of promoting the welfare of women and children.

ARTICLE 157. The State, in order to improve national health, shall establish extensive services for sanitation and health protection, and a system of public medical service.

CHAPTER XIV. ENFORCEMENT AND AMENDMENT OF THE CONSTITUTION

ARTICLE 170. The term "law," as used in this Constitution, shall denote any legislative bill that shall have been passed by the Legislative Yuan and promulgated by the President of the Republic.

ARTICLE 171. Laws that are in conflict with the Constitution shall be null and void.

When doubt arises as to whether or not a law is in conflict with the Constitution, interpretation thereon shall be made by the Judicial Yuan.

ARTICLE 172. Ordinances that are in conflict with the Constitution or with laws shall be null and void.

ARTICLE 173. The Constitution shall be interpreted by the Judicial Yuan.

ARTICLE 174. Amendments to the Constitution shall be made in accordance with one of the following procedures:

(1) Upon the proposal of one-fifth of the total number of the Delegates to the National Assembly and

by a resolution of three-fourths of the Delegates
present at a meeting having a quorum of two-
thirds of the entire Assembly, the Constitution
may be amended.

(2) Upon the proposal of one-fourth of the Members
of the Legislative Yuan and by a resolution of
three-fourths of the Members present at a meeting
having a quorum of three-fourths of the members
of the Yuan, an amendment may be drawn up
and submitted to the National Assembly by way of
referendum. Such a proposed amendment to the
Constitution shall be publicly published half a
year before the National Assembly convenes.

ARTICLE 175. Whenever necessary, enforcement procedures in regard to any matter prescribed in this Constitution shall be separately provided by law.

The preparatory procedures for the enforcement of this
Constitution shall be decided upon by the same National
Assembly which shall have adopted this Constitution.

— Reading No. 21 —

SINO-AMERICAN MUTUAL
DEFENSE TREATY, 1955 [21]

*In December 1953, the Republic of China proposed to
the United States the conclusion of a mutual security
treaty between the two countries. The negotiations were
doubtless accelerated somewhat by the Communist attacks
on the offshore islands beginning in early September 1954.
The treaty was signed at Washington on December 2,
1954, and ratifications were exchanged at Taipei on
March 3, 1955, on which date the treaty came into effect.*

✓   ✓   ✓

[21] *China Handbook, 1955-56* (Taipei, 1955), pp. 250-253.

ARTICLE I. The Parties undertake, as set forth in the Charter of the United Nations, to settle any international dispute in which they may be involved by peaceful means in such a manner that international peace, security and justice are not endangered and to refrain in their international relations from the threat or use of force in any manner inconsistent with the Purposes of the United Nations.

ARTICLE II. In order more effectively to achieve the objective of this Treaty, the Parties separately and jointly by self-help and mutual aid will maintain and develop their individual and collective capacity to resist armed attack and Communist subversive activities directed from without against their territorial integrity and political stability.

ARTICLE III. The Parties undertake to strengthen their free institutions and to cooperate with each other in the development of economic progress and social well-being and to further their individual and collective efforts towards these ends.

ARTICLE IV. The Parties, through their foreign ministers or their deputies, will consult together from time to time regarding the implementation of this Treaty.

ARTICLE V. Each Party recognizes that an armed attack in the West Pacific area on the territories of either of the Parties would be dangerous to its own peace and safety and declares that it would act to meet the common dangers in accordance with its constitutional processes.

Any such armed attack and all measures taken as a result thereof shall be immediately reported to the Security Council of the United Nations. Such measures shall be terminated when the Security Council has taken the measures necessary to restore and maintain international peace and security.

ARTICLE VI. For the purposes of Articles II and V, the term "territorial" and "territories" shall mean in respect of the Republic of China, Taiwan and the Pescadores; and in respect of the United States of America, the island territories in the West Pacific under its jurisdiction. The provisions of Articles II and V will be applicable to such other territories as may be determined by mutual agreement.

ARTICLE VII. The government of the Republic of China

grants, and the Government of the United States of
America accepts, the right to dispose such United States
land, air and sea forces in and about Taiwan and the
Pescadores as may be required for their defense, as determined by mutual agreement.

ARTICLE VIII. This Treaty does not affect and shall not
be interpreted as affecting in any way the rights and
obligations of the Parties under the Charter of the United
Nations or the responsibility of the United Nations for the
maintenance of international peace and security.

ARTICLE IX. This Treaty shall be ratified by the Republic
of China and the United States of America in accordance
with their respective constitutional processes and will
come into force when instruments of ratification thereof
have been exchanged by them at Taipei.

ARTICLE X. This Treaty shall remain in force indefinitely. Either Party may terminate it one year after
notice has been given to the other party. . . .

— Reading No. 22 —

"AMERICA'S POLICY TOWARD
THE CHINESE PEOPLE,"
AUGUST 11, 1958[22]

*On August 11, 1958, the U.S. Department of State is-
sued an official memorandum on China policy to all
United States diplomatic missions abroad. This document
was later published as a pamphlet carrying both English
and Chinese versions, and disseminated widely. The complete English text of this memorandum follows.*

✓   ✓   ✓

[22] "America's Policy toward the Chinese People," (n.p., n.d.),
    pp. 1-9. Minor changes have been made in this text to
    eliminate obvious typographical errors.

Policy towards Communist China has been an important issue since the Communists came to power there, and it is of critical significance to the United States and the Free World today. In the United States the issue is a very real one to the vast majority of the people. As a result of Korean and Chinese Communist aggression in Korea, the United States suffered 142,000 casualties, bringing tragedy to communities all over the country. Nevertheless, despite the emotions thus engendered and the abhorrence of the American people for the brutality and utter lack of morality of Communist systems, the policy of the United States Government towards China has necessarily been based on objective considerations of national interest. It also reflects a continuing appraisal of all available facts.

Basically the United States policy of not extending diplomatic recognition to the Communist regime in China proceeds from the conviction that such recognition would produce no tangible benefits to the United States or to the Free World as a whole and would be of material assistance to Chinese Communist attempts to extend Communist dominion throughout Asia. It is not an "inflexible" policy which cannot be altered to meet changed conditions. If the situation in the Far East were so to change in its basic elements as to call for a radically different evaluation of the threat Chinese Communist policies pose to United States and Free World security interests, the United States would of course readjust its present policies. However, the course of events in the Far East since the establishment of the Chinese Communist regime in 1949 has thus far confirmed the United States view that its interests and those of the Free World are best served by withholding diplomatic recognition from the regime in Peiping.

The basic considerations on which United States policy toward China rests are twofold. First, the Soviet bloc, of which Communist China is an important part, is engaged in a long-range struggle to destroy the way of life of the free countries of the world and bring about the global dominion of Communism. The Chinese Communist regime has made no secret of its fundamental hostility to the United States and the Free World as a whole nor of its avowed intention to effect their downfall.

Today its defiance of and attacks on the non-Communist world have reached a level of intensity that has not been witnessed since the Korean War. The second basic factor is that East Asia is peculiarly vulnerable to the Communist offensive because of the proximity of the free countries of that area to Communist China, the inexperience in self-government of those which have recently won their independence, their suspicions of the West inherited from their colonial past, and the social, political and economic changes which inevitably accompany their drive toward modernization.

The Chinese Communists see the victory of Communism in Asia as inevitable; and now that they control the vast population and territory of mainland China they are utilizing the advantages these give to encompass their ends. Chinese Communist leaders have shown by their words and their acts that they are not primarily interested in promoting the welfare of their people while living at peace with their neighbors. Their primary purpose is to extend the Communist revolution beyond their borders to the rest of Asia and thence to the rest of the world. Liu Chao-chi, the second-ranking member of the Chinese Communist Party, has said: "The most fundamental and common duty of Communist Party members is to establish Communism and transform the present world into a Communist world." Mao Tse-tung himself has said that his regime's policy is "to give active support to the national independence and liberation movements in countries in Asia, Africa and Latin America." That these are not empty words was shown by Chinese Communist aggression in Korea and provisions of arms and other assistance to the Communist rebels in Indochina.

United States policy in Asia, as elsewhere in the world, is to promote the domestic welfare and to strengthen the independence of free nations. Because of the proximity of many Asian nations to mainland China and the disparity in size and power between them and Communist China, this can be done only if the Communist threat is neutralized. The first need of United States policy in the Far East is to deter Communist aggression, else the free nations would be in grave danger of succumbing to Communist pressures before they had gathered the strength with which to resist them. The United States has sought to accomplish this by military assistance to the nations directly in the path of Chinese Communist expansion—Korea, Taiwan, and Vietnam—and by a system of mutual defense arrangements with other nations of the area. We have been successful in this effort and since 1954 the Chinese Communists have not been able to make further gains through the open use of military force.

The measures the United States and its allies in Asia have taken to preserve the security of the free nations of the area are of vital interest to the other free nations of the world. Loss of the rest of East Asia to Communism could have a disastrous effect on the free world's ability to resist effectively the encroachments of Communism elsewhere. The consequences for Australia and New Zealand would be especially serious. Loss of the islands of the West Pacific and of the Southeast Asian peninsula would isolate these countries and place them in a strategically exposed and dangerous position.

Efforts to halt further Communist expansion cannot be confined to military deterrence alone. Counter-measures against Chinese Communist subversion and political infiltration are equally necessary. This is especially so as, since 1955, Peiping has increasingly resorted to propaganda, subversion, "people's" diplomacy, and political maneuvering in its dealings with its Asian neighbors. Peiping seeks to win by this means what it apparently does not dare attempt through military conquest. The United States therefore considers that in preserving the peace and security of Asia it is as important to be alert to the threat of subversion as to that of open military attack.

In the effort to block Peiping's attempts to extend Communist rule in Asia the withholding of diplomatic recognition is an important factor. The extension of diplomatic recognition by a great power normally carries with it not only increased access to international councils but enhanced international standing and prestige as well. Denial of recognition on the other hand is a positive handicap to the regime affected and one which makes it that much the more difficult for it to pursue its foreign policies with success. One basic purpose of United States

non-recognition of Communist China is to deny it
these advantages and to that extent limit its ability to
threaten the security of the area.

In the case of China there are special considerations
which influence United States policy with regard to
recognition. For one thing, although the Chinese Communists have seized the preponderant bulk of China,
they have not completed their conquest of the country.
The generally recognized legitimate government of China
continues to exist and in Taiwan is steadily developing
its political, economic and military strength. The government of the Republic of China controls the strategic
island of Taiwan and through its possession of a sizeable
military force—one of the largest on the side of the Free
World in Asia—presents a significant deterrent to renewed Chinese Communist aggression. Recognition of
Communist China by the United States would seriously
cripple, if not destroy altogether, that government. On
the other hand, continued United States recognition and
support of the Republic of China enables it to challenge
the claim of the Chinese Communists to represent the
Chinese people and keeps alive the hopes of those Chinese
who are determined eventually to free their country of
Communist rule.

Recognition of Communist China by the United States
would have an adverse effect on the other free governments of Asia which could be disastrous to the cause of
the Free World in that part of the world. Those nations
which are closely allied to the United States and are
striving to maintain their independence on the perimeter
of Chinese Communist power, especially Korea and
Vietnam, would be profoundly confused and demoralized. They would interpret such action as abandonment of
their cause by the United States. They might reason that
their only hope for survival lay in desperate measures,
not caring whether these threatened the peace of the area
and the world. Governments further removed from the
borders of China would see in American recognition of
Communist China the first step in the withdrawal of the
United States from the Far East. Without the support of
the United States they would be unable long to defy the
will of Peiping; and some would probably conclude that
their wisest course would be speedily to seek the best

terms obtainable from Peiping. Needless to say, these developments would place the entire Free World position in Asia in the gravest peril.

Another special consideration in the case of China is that large and influential "overseas" Chinese communities exist in most of the countries of Southeast Asia.

The efforts of these countries to build healthy free societies and to develop their economies would be seriously retarded if these communities were to fall under the sway of the Chinese Communists; and a grave threat of Communist subversion through those overseas communities would arise. Recognition of Communist China by the United States and the decline in the fortunes of the United States and the decline in the fortunes of the Republic of China which would inevitably result, would have such a profound psychological effect on the overseas Chinese that it would make inevitable the transfer of the loyalties of large numbers to the Communist side. This in turn would undermine the ability of the host countries to resist the pressures tending to promote the expansion of Chinese Communist influence and power.

Still another factor which must be considered in the case of China is the effect which recognition of the Communist regime would have on the United Nations. Recognition of Peiping by the United States would inevitably lead to the seating of Peiping in that body. In the view of the United States this would vitiate, if not destroy, the United Nations as an instrument for the maintenance of international peace. The Korean War was the first and most important effort to halt aggression through collective action in the United Nations. For Communist China, one of the parties against which the effort of the United Nations was directed, to be seated in the United Nations while still unpurged of its aggression and defying the will of the United Nations in Korea, would amount to a confession of failure on the part of the United Nations and would greatly reduce the prospects for future successful action by the United Nations against aggression. Moreover, the Republic of China is a charter member in good standing of the United Nations and its representatives there have contributed importantly to the constructive work of that organization. If the representatives of the Chinese Communist regime were to be seated in their place and given China's veto in the Security Council, the ability of that body in the future to discharge the responsibility it has under the charter for the maintaining of international peace and security would be seriously impaired.

Those who advocate recognition of the Chinese Communists often assume that by the standards of international law applied to such cases the Peiping regime is "entitled" to diplomatic recognition. In the view of the United States diplomatic recognition is a privilege and not a right. Moreover, the United States considers that diplomatic recognition is an instrument of national policy which it is both its right and its duty to use in the enlightened self-interest of the nation. However, there is reason to doubt that even by the tests often cited in international law the Chinese Communist regime qualifies for diplomatic recognition. It does not rule all China, and there is a substantial force in being which contests its claim to do so. The Chinese Communist Party which holds mainland China in its grip is a tiny minority comprising less than two percent of the Chinese people, and the regimentation, brutal repression, and forced sacrifices that have characterized its rule have resulted in extensive popular unrest. To paraphrase Thomas Jefferson's dictum, this regime certainly does not represent "the will of the populace, substantially declared." Finally, it has shown no intention to honor its international obligations. One of its first acts was to abrogate the treaties of the Republic of China except those it chose to continue. On assuming power it carried out a virtual confiscation without compensation of the properties of foreign nationals, including immense British investments notwithstanding the United Kingdom's prompt recognition of it. It has failed to honor various commitments entered into since, including various provisions of the Korean Armistice and the Geneva Accord on Viet-nam and Laos as well as the "agreed" announcement of September, 1955, by which it pledged itself to permit all Americans in China to return home "expeditiously."

The United States policy toward recognition of Communist China is then based on a carefully considered judgment of the national interest. Non-recognition of

Peiping coupled with continued recognition and support of the Republic of China facilitates the accomplishment of United States policy objectives in the Far East. Recognition of Peiping would seriously hinder accomplishment of these objectives and would facilitate the advance of Communist power in Asia.

In the process of determining its policy toward China the United States has taken into account the various statements and arguments advanced by proponents of extending diplomatic recognition to Peiping. One of the most commonly advanced reasons for recognition is that reality must be "recognized" and 600 million people cannot be "ignored." While superficially appealing both statements themselves overlook the realities of the situation. United States policy is, of course, based on full appreciation of the fact that the Chinese Communist regime is currently in control of mainland China. However, it is not necessary to have diplomatic relations with a regime in order to deal with it. Without extending diplomatic recognition the United States has participated in extended negotiations with Chinese Communist representatives, in the Korean and Indochina armistice negotiations and more recently in the ambassadorial talks in Geneva. Similarly, United States policy in no sense "ignores" the existence and the aspirations of the Chinese people. Its attitude toward the people of China remains what it historically has been, one of friendship and sympathetic understanding. It is nonetheless clear that our friendship for the Chinese people must not be permitted to blind us to the threat to our security which the Communist regime in China now presents. Moreover, the United States is convinced that the Chinese Communist regime does not represent the true will or aspirations of the Chinese people and that our policy of withholding recognition from it is in actuality in their ultimate interest.

It is sometimes contended that by recognition of Communist China it would be possible to exert leverage on the Peiping regime which might ultimately be successful in weakening or even breaking the bond with Moscow. Unfortunately, there is no evidence to support this belief and there are important reasons why it is unlikely; the alliance between Moscow and Peiping is one of long

standing; it traces its origin to the very founding of the
Chinese Communist Party in 1921, in which representatives of the Comintern played an important role.

It is based on a common ideology and on mutually-held
objectives with respect to the non-Communist world. All
recent evidence points to the closeness of the tie between
the Chinese Communists and the USSR rather than in
the other direction. The Chinese Communists were out-
spoken in championing the armed intervention of the
Soviets in Hungary and have given unqualified endorse-
ment to the execution of Nagy and the other leaders of
the Hungarian revolt. They were also leaders in the
recent Communist bloc attack on Yugoslavia for its
attempts to pursue national policies independent of
Kremlin control. These and other facts make it apparent
that the two partners in the Sino-Soviet alliance clearly
realize their mutual dependence and attach great importance to bloc unity vis-a-vis the Free World.

Furthermore, the alliance with the USSR has a special
importance for the Chinese Communists since it provides
them with a dependable source of arms and military supplies. The Chinese Communist leaders, including Mao
Tse-tung himself, came to power through their command
of military force. They are therefore keenly conscious
of the importance of military force to keep themselves in
power against domestic and external opposition and to
achieve the goals of their foreign policy. It is scarcely
credible that they would dare risk any course of action
which could lead to loss of their source of military supplies. For this reason alone, it would seem unrealistic
to believe that recognition of Peiping by the United States
or any other leading nation would have the effect of
tempting the Chinese Communists to play a "Titoist"
role.

In fact the opposite is quite likely to be the result.
Were the United States to grant diplomatic recognition to
Peiping—with all that this would entail by way of enhanced international prestige—its leaders would most
likely feel confirmed in the correctness of their policies
and the advantages of continued close cooperation with
Moscow.

It is often alleged that recognition of Communist China
is a necessary step in expanding trade relations with that

country. For the United States this is of course not a consideration, since the United States embargoes trade with Peiping under the Trading with the Enemy Act as a result of the Korean War. But even for countries which do desire to expand trade with mainland China, the facts do not support the contention that trade is dependent on recognition. To the contrary, Great Britain, which recognized Communist China in 1950, has found that she buys more goods from Communist China than Communist China buys from her. West Germany on the other hand does not recognize Peiping and enjoys a favorable trade balance with the mainland China. In any case, trade opportunities with Communist China are severely limited by a shortage of foreign exchange which is likely to persist for many years to come. Moreover, such trade would always be at the mercy of Communist policies. Peiping uses trade as a means of exerting pressure on the trading partner whenever it deems this to be expedient. A striking example is the case of Japan, where the Chinese Communists recently retaliated against Japanese refusal to make certain political concessions by cutting off all trade and even cancelling contracts which had already been entered into. It would therefore seem that over the long run the advantages of trade with Peiping will prove more ephemeral than real.

An argument often heard is that the Chinese Communists are here "to stay"; that they will have to be recognized sooner or later; and that it would be the course of wisdom to bow to the inevitable now rather than be forced to do so ungracefully at a later date. It is true that there is no reason to believe that the Chinese Communist regime is on the verge of collapse; but there is equally no reason to accept its present rule in mainland China as permanent. In fact, unmistakable signs of dissatisfaction and unrest in Communist China have appeared in the "ideological remoulding" and the mass campaign against "rightists" which have been in progress during the past year. Dictatorships often create an illusion of permanence from the very fact that they suppress and still all opposition, and that of the Chinese Communists is no exception to this rule. The United States holds the view that Communism's rule in China is not permanent and that it one day will pass. By withholding

diplomatic recognition from Peiping it seeks to hasten
that passing.

In public discussions of China policy one of the proposals that has attracted widest attention is that known
as the "Two Chinas Solution." Briefly, advocates of this
arrangement propose that the Chinese Communist regime
be recognized as the government of mainland China
while the government at Taipei remains as the legal government of Taiwan. They argue that this approach to the
Chinese problem has the merit of granting the Communists only what they already control while retaining
for the Free World the militarily strategic bastion of
Taiwan. However, it overlooks or ignores certain facts of
basic importance. The Republic of China would not accept
any diminution of its sovereignty over China and could
be expected to resist such an arrangement with all the
means at its disposal. If a "Two Chinas Solution" were
to be forcefully imposed against its will, that government's effectiveness as a loyal ally to the Free World
cause would be destroyed. Peiping too would reject such
an arrangement. In fact over the past year Chinese Communist propaganda has repeatedly and stridently denounced the "Two Chinas" concept and, ironically, has
been accusing the United States government of attempting
to put it into effect. Peiping attaches great importance to
the eventual acquisition of Taiwan and has consistently
reserved what it calls its "right" to seize Taiwan by
force if other means fail. There is no prospect that it
would ever acquiesce in any arrangement which would
lead to the permanent detachment of Taiwan from China.

The "Two Chinas" concept is bitterly opposed by both
Peiping and Taipei. Hence, even if such a solution could
be imposed by outside authority, it would not be a stable
one. Constant policing would be required to avert its
violent overthrow by one side or the other.

It is sometimes said that non-recognition of Peiping
tends to martyrize the Chinese Communists, thereby
enabling them to pose, especially before Asian neutralists, as an innocent and injured party. It would be
impossible to deny that there is some truth in this. But
this disadvantage is far outweighed by the opposite
course. It is surely better that some neutralists, who are
either unable or unwilling to comprehend the threat

inherent in Chinese Communist policies, mistakenly consider Peiping unjustly treated than that the allies of the United States in Asia, who are the first line of defense against Chinese Communist expansion, should be confused and demoralized by what to them could only appear to be a betrayal of the common sense.

Forty-five non-Communist countries recognize the Republic of China. Only nineteen have recognized Peiping, and most of these did so before the Korean War in 1950. Recognition by a leading Free World nation would therefore be interpreted as an important victory for the Chinese Communists, as a sign of Free World reluctance to stand up to Communist pressures, and as damaging evidence of a serious difference of opinion within the Free World concerning the problem of how to deal with the expansionist forces of international Communism. It would have an especially serious effect in the Far East where the Free World nations most directly exposed to Chinese Communist expansionist pressures would be dismayed and confused and some would no doubt be tempted to follow suit for fear of being left in the face of Communist power. Nations in other areas of the world whose governments are less conscious of the critical nature of the situation in the Far East and less immediately affected by developments in that area might follow the example thus set. The inevitable consequence of recognition of the Chinese Communist regime by other Free Nations would be greatly to enhance its prestige, influence, and power and to make more difficult the effort to maintain Free World security interests in the Pacific area.

A SHORT BIBLIOGRAPHY

Chiang Kai-shek, *Soviet Russia in China* (New York, 1957).

China Yearbook, 1957-1958 (Taipei, 1958).

H. G. Creel, *Chinese Thought from Confucius to Mao Tse-tung* (Chicago, 1953).

G. B. Cressey, *Land of the 500 Million: A Geography of China* (New York, 1955).

T. Dennett, *Americans in Eastern Asia* (New York, 1922).

Y. Gluckstein, *Mao's China* (Boston, 1957).

M. Granet, *Chinese Civilization,* transl. by K. Innes and M. Brailsford (New York, 1951).

A. W. Griswold, *The Far Eastern Policy of the United States* (New York, 1938).

Han Lih-wu, *Taiwan Today* (Taipei, 1958).

Hu Shih, *The Chinese Renaissance* (Chicago, 1934).

E. R. Hughes, *The Invasion of China by the Western World* (London, 1937).

A. W. Hummel, ed., *Eminent Chinese of the Ch'ing Period (1644-1912)* (Washington, 1944).

E. Hunter, *Brain-washing in Red China* (New York, 1951).

K. S. Latourette, *A History of Modern China* (London, 1956).

K. S. Latourette, *The Chinese: Their History and Culture* (New York, 1946).

Li, Chien-nung, *The Political History of China 1840-1928,* Ed. and transl. by Ssu-yu Teng and Jeremy Ingalls (Princeton, 1956).

P. M. A. Linebarger, Djang Chu and A. W. Burks, *Far Eastern Governments and Politics, China and Japan* (New York, 1954).

H. F. MacNair, ed., *Modern Chinese History, Selected Readings* (Shanghai, 1923).

H. F. MacNair, *The Real Conflict Between China and Japan* (Chicago, 1938).

188

H. F. MacNair and D. F. Lach, *Modern Far Eastern International Relations* (New York, 1950).

Mao Tse-tung, *Selected Works of Mao Tse-tung* (London, 1954).

F. H. Michael and G. E. Taylor, *The Far East in the Modern World* (New York, 1956).

H. B. Morse, *The International Relations of the Chinese Empire* (London, 1910-1918).

F. W. Price, Transl., *San Min Chu I, The Three Principles of the People* (Shanghai, 1927).

A. F. Raper, Han-sheng Chuan, Shao-hsing Chen, *Urban and Industrial Taiwan—Crowded and Resourceful* (Taipei, 1954).

D. N. Rowe, *China among the Powers* (New York, 1945).

E. Swisher, *China's Management of the American Barbarians* (New Haven, 1951).

Hui-sun Tang, *Land Reform in Free China* (Taipei, 1954).

P. S. H. Tang, *Communist China Today: Domestic and Foreign Policies* (New York, 1957).

Teng Ssu-yu and J. K. Fairbank, *China's Response to the West: A Documentary Survey (1839-1923)* (Cambridge, 1953).

U.S. Congress, House Committee on Foreign Affairs, *Communism in China* (Washington, 1948).

United States Relations with China, with Special Reference to the Period 1944-1949 (Washington, 1949).

H. M. Vinacke, *A History of the Far East in Modern Times* (New York, 1950).

R. L. Walker, *China Under Communism: The First Five Years* (New Haven, 1955).

INDEX

VAN NOSTRAND ANVIL BOOKS already published

DATE DUE

GAYLORD			PRINTED IN U.S.A.